THE COMPLETE ROUND-THE-WORLD HORS D'OEUVRES BOOK

"... is a wonderful compendium of all the canapes, dips, spreads, appetizers, quiches, pastry, hibachi and skewer and chafing-dish recipes for all kinds of tastes from everywhere for any occasion. . . ."

(Park East)

"... should provide a shot in the arm for hostesses tired of the usual spread-on-a-cracker appetizer."

(Chattanooga Times)

"THE COMPLETE ROUND THE WORLD HORS D'OEUVRES BOOK offers the most comprehensive collection of appetizers. . . ."

(Promenade)

"From Shish Kabob, Turkish style, to hot crabmeat canapes, cocktail hour becomes the talk of the town for the tidbit gourmet."

(The Hartford Times)

"MOUTH-WATERING READING."

(Chattanooga Times)

THE COMPLETE
ROUND THE WORLD
HORS D'OEUVRES BOOK

By Myra Waldo

PAPERBACK LIBRARY
New York

PAPERBACK LIBRARY EDITION

First Printing: August, 1967
Second Printing: December, 1969

Copyright © 1964 by Myra Waldo Schwartz

All rights reserved

Library of Congress Catalog Card Number 64-19240

This Paperback Library Edition is published
by arrangement with Doubleday & Company, Inc.

Paperback Library is a division of Coronet Communications, Inc.
Its trademark, consisting of the words "Paperback Library" accom-
panied by an open book, is registered in the United States Patent
Office. *Coronet Communications, Inc., 315 Park Avenue South,
New York, N.Y. 10010.*

CONTENTS

INTRODUCTION

"The beginning is half the undertaking."

—Greek Proverb

THE INVITATION "have a drink" has come to mean an expression of hospitality all over the world. Today's fashion for easier living seems to rely on the cocktail party as the ideal form of entertaining.

Perfectly served drinks are important, of course, but the truly successful party is dependent on the hors d'oeuvres accompanying the drinks.

Hors d'oeuvre is the universally accepted term for a food that stimulates the appetite. It can be anything as simple as a nibble of spicy cheese, or as elaborate as a galantine, but in whatever form, it is intended to pique the appetite and excite the eye.

The cocktail party is the perfect way to entertain large numbers of guests, or in the alternative, just a few intimate friends. Your choice of hors d'oeuvres, of course, should depend on the number of people invited and the facilities for service. It is better to have two perfectly prepared hors d'oeuvres than a myriad of indifferent ones. In American terminology today, hors d'oeuvres include canapés or any "finger foods" that can be picked up without the aid of a fork, dips, spreads, pâtés, pastries, and in fact anything that is served with drinks.

For the straight cocktail party, that is, without dinner to follow, it is advisable to have a generous and varied assortment. But balance is important. Plan the selection so that there are several cold appetizers, two or more hot dishes, bowls of nuts, and of course, for the dieters, some crisp raw vegetables. Try not to duplicate the ingredients—for example, don't have two chicken hors d'oeuvres.

Always serve the cold appetizers cold, and hot ones hot. There is nothing as tasteless as a tepid hors d'oeuvre that was intended to be served hot. If you have a chafing dish or hot tray, serve the appetizers directly from it. If not, place only a few hot hors d'oeuvres on a heated serving dish, and refill it frequently.

7

Appetizers should always be prepared small or soft enough so that a knife is not required. It is generally a good idea to provide small plates and, for the more elaborate preparations, forks. Set up small tables in various parts of the room, particularly if there is not enough seating room. It is difficult to balance a plate and glass at the same time, and the tables will provide a resting place for one or the other, temporarily at least.

The proper quantity needed requires careful consideration. You can assume the average guest will consume a minimum of six appetizers, but you must allow for more, particularly if the appetizers are quite small. If guests are coming at different times, keep a small assortment in reserve for the later guests.

The hors d'oeuvres may be arranged on a large table, or on several small tables in different places, depending on the size of the room. Or if you have sufficient help, they may be passed on platters. Just don't attempt more than you can handle comfortably. The secret of relaxed entertaining is organization, and the ambiance of the occasion depends on the hostess.

If your cocktail party is a success, and of course it should be, you might find that some people, particularly intimate friends, stay late, so it is a good idea to have a casserole or some other easily prepared dish in the refrigerator or freezer. With such a stand-by, you'll be able to extend your hospitality without too much trouble.

The cocktail hour before a dinner presents a slightly different problem. You may serve the appetizers in the living room, and then omit a first course at the table, if you wish. Be sure the hors d'oeuvres complement the rest of the meal. Thus, if the main course is comparatively light, (fish, for example) the appetizers may be rich and savory, but don't use ingredients similar to those used in the entrée.

Hors d'oeuvres, of course, may also be served as a first course at the table, in the French or Italian (antipasto) style. It may be an assortment, such as pâté, marinated vegetables, fish, shrimp, etc. If it is a well-prepared, attractively arranged plate, it will make a hit.

The freezer can play an important role in the preparation of hors d'oeuvres. Many of the recipes included in the book can be prepared in advance, frozen, then thawed, and re-heated when needed, whether for a party or the unexpected guest.

I have included a very wide range of the most delicious and unusual appetizers from all over the world. It should help to make entertaining easier and far more interesting. A special section on quiches is also included; these delicious open unsweetened tarts are perfect for cocktail parties when prepared as individual tarts or cut into small wedges. They are equally good when cut into larger pieces and served as a first course at the dinner table.

There are hot appetizers, cold preparations, pastries, some filled, others plain, hors d'oeuvres made of fish, chicken, meat and vegetables, and there are the rich pâtés of various types. Many of the hors d'oeuvres are also ideal as a first course. Join the trend toward easier entertaining with complete confidence, assured that your hors d'oeuvres are interesting and different.

Myra Waldo

THE HISTORY OF HORS D'OEUVRES

No ONE seems to know exactly when, or even how, these appetizing tidbits evolved. Japanese cookbooks—primitive but nevertheless cookbooks—contain specific references to pickled fish, intended to be served before a meal. One of these Japanese books has been authenticated as having been written about 3000 B.C. If so, appetizers are approximately 5000 years old.

At elaborate parties held in Athens as early as 350 B.C., platters of foods wrapped in pale-green vine leaves were served before the banquet; these were obviously the forerunner of Greece's modern dolmas. At the height of Grecian power and influence, appetizers were called "provocatives" to drinking. They also included caviar, a variety of olives, spicy cheese, pickled octopus and roasted pistachio nuts, a selection which would be perfectly acceptable today, although most Americans would gladly forego the octopus.

In Persia, during the time of Queen Esther, food became increasingly important, and appetizers became such a cult or rage that prizes were awarded for new recipes. It is thought that kebobs, skewered foods, originated during this period. Kebobs are now a standard appetizer throughout the world, especially in the Near and Middle East. In southeast Asia they are called saté, and flavored somewhat differently, and the same is true in France, where they are called brochettes.

In early Roman days, appetizers were called gustatio, from which we derive gustatory, having to do with the sensation of taste. (Gustatio, therefore, might be translated as tasters, or appetizers.) It was considered appropriate to serve as many as fifty different kinds at a formal dinner, but cost was seldom a consideration in those days. Heliogabalus, the Roman emperor, had little regard for expense if he thought there was any delicacy which might tempt his capricious appetite. He maintained, at Rome's expense, a set of fishing boats to catch eels. The eel roe was treated and served much as caviar is now. The price per serving was probably higher

11

than fresh caviar is today, but the emperor sought only newer and more expensive appetizers.

The extravagance of Lucullus, the outstanding gourmet of Roman times, knew no limits, and no effort was spared to procure some delicacy for his table. To be invited to a banquet by Lucullus was an experience—as scores of Roman writers have told us. It was not unusual to spend the equivalent of a thousand dollars per person on the cost of food. However, even when Lucullus dined alone, his chef was expected to provide a meal costing ten thousand dollars. To such an extent have richness of food and disregard for cost been associated with his name that even today "Lucullan" refers to an extravagant dish or repast. In his continuing search for appetizing delicacies, Lucullus was not one to concern himself with the high cost of living. Unusual appetizers were his particular favorite, and he dispatched explorers to all corners of the then known world. They returned with obscure items—eggs from the rarest of birds, exotic fish from the ocean's depths, herbs and spices never before seen in Imperial Rome, and fish roe carried by series of messengers so as to reach this insatiable gourmet as quickly as possible. Peacocks' tongues were then considered a great appetizer, but peacocks were none too plentiful. For a year or more, thousands of scouts rounded up every possible bird; the colorful birds were dispatched, the tongues removed and the remainder of the bird discarded so that Lucullus and friends could dine on the tongues of peacocks.

After the collapse of the Roman Empire people still enjoyed food, but the days of great extravagance were past. In medieval Venice, elaborate meals were served on special occasions, and various appetizers were offered to the guests waiting for the many-coursed meal, much as at a modern pre-dinner cocktail party. It is believed that today's cocktail party had its beginning in a Greek town in Italy called Sybaris. It became the custom to invite people to a long-run drinking party that went on for days, until the exhausted guests finally dragged themselves home for a long, long sleep. It was the tradition in Sybaris that no regular meals be served during the continuous drinking party, only small tidbits and snacks being offered. Unquestionably today's cocktail parties of three or four hours represent a vast improvement over the

12

Sybaritic system. Our sympathies go out to a hostess of those days.

In modern Italy, antipasto is the present-day appetizer equivalent of the extravagances of bygone days. Antipasto may be quite simple—just a spicy mixture of vegetables or, more elaborate, with sardines or shrimp. It may be crisp, fresh vegetables served with the classic bagna cauda sauce made of garlic, olive oil, butter and mashed anchovies; in some parts of Italy stuffed vegetables (such as peppers, eggplant and tomatoes) are the great favorites. But whatever it is, antipasto is intended to, and does, pique the appetite for the meal to follow.

The mandarins of ancient China were great enthusiasts of the culinary art, and did all they could to develop the skills of their cooks. A competent chef of that period had a repertoire of over a thousand dishes, and was not expected to repeat a given preparation in a year. Ti wei ping, Chinese appetizers, comprise an enormous selection, many of which are familiar to anyone who has dined in an authentic Chinese restaurant. A classic selection might include smoked meats, fish balls, dried abalone, shrimp and the like. In more modern usage, Chinese appetizers usually consist of fried shrimp, thin slices of roast pork, fried stuffed dumplings, egg (or spring) rolls, spareribs and shrimp toast.

The Tartars were a nomadic people, wandering over the face of central Asia, with occasional forays into eastern Europe. When possible, the Tartars roasted meat over an open fire, but if time did not permit, they enjoyed it raw. From these hardy nomads, it is thought, we derive an outstanding appetizer, steak tartare, tiny balls of raw meat. The Russians later embellished it with caviar, making it even more delicious.

In all Scandinavian countries today, smoked fish are outstanding favorites as appetizers. The hearty Viking ancestors of the Scandinavians were responsible for the delicacy and flavor achieved by smoking fish, although they were not thinking so much in terms of appetizers as they were of a method of preventing fish from spoiling on long sea voyages. The Vikings hit upon smoking as the perfect way of keeping fish, and we are the beneficiaries of their skills, not to mention the pleasure of eating smoked fish.

Smoked fish still plays a vital part in the classic smörgåsbord of Sweden, but it is a simple, rather meager presentation that doesn't also include cheese, shellfish, meat, salads and the like. In Denmark the Swedish smörgåsbord is modified; instead of selecting items from platters, the smorrebrod consists of beautifully arranged open sandwiches of shrimp, fish, meat, eggs or cheese. In Norway and Finland, too, large assortments of appetizers are the rule, usually cold but sometimes hot.

Dried meats have always been a popular appetizer. In Italy, of course, there is prosciutto, the delicately flavored ham so delicious when eaten plain or with grated pepper, but particularly good with slices of melon or fresh figs. In Switzerland they prepare thin strips of air-dried beef, called bundnerfleisch, of extraordinary delicacy. The Italian equivalent of bundnerfleisch is called bresaola. In Spain they prepare a marvelous cured-ham appetizer, jamón de serrano. Belgium's jambon d'Ardennes is also worthy of special notice.

The Spanish conquistadors, who ultimately changed the food habits of Europe, found many new items in the New World. All of these, in addition to gold wrenched from the Mayans and Incas, found their way back to the Continent. In particular, New World flavorings and spices tempted and delighted the appetites of those who had prudently remained behind. The Spaniards found the avocado, and also guacamole, the favorite appetizer made of avocado.

It is generally agreed that France has made the greatest contribution of any nation to the art of good living, and of fine foods. However, much of the credit must go to Italy, whose chefs revolutionized the Gallic cuisine of the period. During the fifteenth and sixteenth centuries it was the Italians, not the French, who ruled the culinary world. When Catherine de Medici married the Duke of Orléans (who later became King Henry II of France), she brought with her as part of her dowry a group of Italian chefs to teach the French how to cook. The Florentine cooks were the first to show the French the possibility of serving appetizers before the meal. It was about this time that the phrase hors d'oeuvre came into being. Translated literally, it means "outside the work," a French phrase intended to cover foods served, other than the main part of the meal. Other words came into being

14

about the same period. Canapés, little pieces of bread holding an appetizing morsel, are based upon another meaning for the same word, namely a comfortable place to sit, and of course the anchovy or other savory food rest comfortably upon the bread. Amusantes, frivolités and other terms designed to make the eater think that hors d'oeuvres are loads of fun came into existence.

On their own, during the same century, the Russians were evolving another style of appetizers, which they called zakuska. It is very similar to modern appetizers—smoked fish, caviar, small filled pastries, chopped meat mixtures and thirst-inducing salad combinations. With zakuska, the classic drink was, and still is, chilled vodka. I regret to say that on a recent visit to Russia I found the variety greatly diminished, and also the quality.

In modern times all over the world, wherever one may be, the cocktail party is the standard method of having large number of guests. I have been entertained at cocktail parties in all parts of the world, some quite unlikely, including Tahiti, Katmandu, Cuzco, and Srinagar. Two other cocktail parties quickly come to mind. One took place at the foothills of Mount Kilimanjaro in Kenya; it was a "sundowner," a term used in English colonies, and took place before a roaring open fire of baobab logs. The appetizer was a sort of kebob of pieces of fresh liver from an eland (a large antelope) grilled over the fire. I like liver, but I don't enjoy looking at the animal, whose carcass lay at my feet, at the same time. Another distinctive cocktail party took place in Rangoon, Burma; it was a traditional head-shaving (for a boy) and ear-piercing (for a girl) combination ceremony. For both, it signified maturity. For me, it represented another chance to taste the local appetizers, in this case delicious curried pastries.

We are indebted to the inventors of so many delicious dishes, which have been handed down through the centuries.

Almost every nation in the world knows and enjoys appetizers, although by different names:

French:	Hors d'oeuvre
Italian:	Antipasto
Spanish:	Entreméses

Portuguese:	Acepipes
Dutch:	Voorgerechten
German:	Vorspeisen
Scandinavian:	Smörgåsbord, Smorrebrod, Smorgas
Finnish:	Voileipäpöytä
Greek:	Mezedakia
Turkish:	Mezeler
Yugoslavian:	Predjelo
Russian:	Zakuska
Syrian:	Maza
Chinese:	Ti Wei Ping
Japanese:	Ossakeno Sakana O'dobre

DIPS AND SPREADS

DIPS AND SPREADS are actually the basis of "do-it-yourself" canapés, and provide a simplified method of service. They merely require an attractive bowl or other container and small knives, spoons or forks for spreading. For spreads, thinly sliced bread or brioches, toast, pastry, or miniature pancakes may be used as the base. Chips, pretzels, vegetable sticks, toast fingers or crackers are all ideal for dunking into dips. Check the freshness of the chips, etc., before serving. A soggy food that is meant to be crisp should not be used. A few minutes in a hot oven will often restore the desired texture.

Offer contrast in taste and texture when serving dips and spreads, and do not repeat ingredients. For example, if a mixture has cheddar cheese in it, do not use it in any other dip.

Appetizers are enjoyed the world over, and this section features several outstanding preparations. Taramosalata is a delicious Greek hors d'oeuvre, quite like the much more expensive caviar. Lomi lomi, the Hawaiian spread made with chopped smoked salmon, has an excellent flavor, and brandade de morue, a favorite in Southern France, can become your family favorite too. Another classic appetizer of France is le saussoon, made from anchovies and almonds. Shellfish

16

hors d'oeuvres are liked around the globe, but particularly worthy of note is Indonesia's sambal oedang, made with shrimp.

Dips and spreads are an American way of serving appetizers, on a sort of do-it-yourself basis that is a natural result of our obvious lack of domestic help. However, in the vast majority of cases, the preparation originated overseas, and it is only the method of presenting the dish that is truly American.

RUSSIAN CAVIAR DIP

¼ pound cream cheese	2 tablespoons grated onions
1 cup sour cream	½ cup red or black caviar

Beat the cheese, sour cream and onions until very smooth. Blend in the caviar. Serve with crisp crackers or buttered toast fingers.

Makes about 2 cups.

GREEK RED CAVIAR SPREAD

3 slices white bread, trimmed	1/3 cup finely chopped onions
1 cup water	¼ cup lemon juice
1 8-ounce jar red caviar	¾ cup olive oil

Soak the bread in the water, drain, mash smooth and squeeze dry. Combine the bread, caviar, onions and lemon juice in a bowl. Mix with a wooden spoon until smooth. Very gradually mix in the olive oil until a pale pink. Chill. Serve in a bowl, with thinly sliced French or Italian bread.

Makes about 2¼ cups.

RED-CAVIAR DIP

1 3-ounce package cream cheese	2 tablespoons grated onions
½ cup sour cream	¼ pound red caviar

Mash the cheese, then beat in the sour cream until light and fluffy. Mix in the onions and caviar. Serve with potato chips, crisp crackers or toast squares.

Makes about 1 cup.

TARAMOSALATA (Greek Mullet Caviar)

5 slices white bread, trimmed
1 cup cold water
¼ cup grated onions
½ pound tarama (Greek dried
  red-mullet roe)

1 cup sesame or olive oil
¼ cup lemon juice

Soak the bread in the water, then squeeze out the excess water. With an electric mixer or rotary beater, beat the soaked bread until smooth. Add the onions, beating until fluffy, then beat in 1 tablespoon of the tarama at a time. Continue beating for a few minutes after all has been added, then alternate the oil and lemon, drop by drop, beating steadily. Continue beating until mixture is creamy and a pale pink. Heap in a bowl, chill, then garnish with chopped onions and black olives, if desired. Serve with French or Italian bread.

Makes about 3 cups.

Variation: Molded Taramosalata

Soften 2 envelopes (tablespoons) gelatin in ¼ cup cold water, then place over hot water and stir until dissolved. Mix in the taramosalata, pour into an oiled 1-quart mold and chill until firm. Unmold onto a chilled serving dish.

SARDINE SPREAD

2 3¼-ounce cans sardines
¼ teaspoon A.1. Sauce
1 tablespoon ketchup

¼ cup sour cream
2 teaspoons prepared horseradish
Paprika

Mash sardines; mix in the A.1. Sauce, ketchup, sour cream and horseradish. Sprinkle with paprika and serve with crisp crackers or toast fingers. Makes about 1 cup.

SARDINHAS (Sardine Hors d'Oeuvre Spread, Portuguese Style)

1 7½-ounce can sardines
3 tablespoons finely chopped onions
2 tablespoons chopped pimientos
4 slices crisp bacon, crumbled
1 tablespoon finely chopped mushrooms
1 tablespoon finely chopped celery
1 tablespoon chopped Brazil nuts or almonds
¼ teaspoon freshly ground black pepper
¼ teaspoon paprika
½ cup mayonnaise
¼ cup ketchup
2 tablespoons A.1. Sauce
2 tablespoons lemon juice
1 teaspoon prepared mustard

Mash the undrained sardines; mix in the onions, pimientos, bacon, mushrooms, celery, nuts, pepper and paprika. Form into a mound on a serving dish.

Mix together the mayonnaise, ketchup, A.1. Sauce, lemon juice and mustard. Turn into a small bowl and place on the serving dish. Serve with fresh toast squares or melba rounds. The sardine mixture should be spread on first, then covered with the dressing. Makes about 1½ cups.

SPICY SARDINE SPREAD

¼ pound cream cheese
3 tablespoons heavy cream
2 teaspoons prepared mustard
3 tablespoons grated onions
¼ teaspoon freshly ground black pepper
1 7½-ounce can skinless boneless sardines, drained and mashed

Beat the cheese, cream, mustard and onions until very smooth. Blend in the pepper and sardines. Heap in a bowl and chill. Serve with potato or corn chips or toast fingers. Makes about 1¼ cups.

TUNA DIP

2 7-ounce cans tuna fish
½ pound cream cheese
¼ cup dry sherry
¼ cup sour cream
1 tablespoon grated onions
3 tablespoons chili sauce
1 teaspoon Worcestershire sauce
¼ teaspoon freshly ground black pepper
2 tablespoons minced parsley

19

Drain and flake the tuna fish. Beat the cheese smooth, then blend in the sherry, sour cream, onions, chili sauce, Worcestershire sauce, pepper and parsley. Mix in the tuna fish, taste for seasoning. Heap in a bowl. Serve with potato chips, crisp crackers or toast squares. Makes about 3 cups.

SALMON DIP

1 7¾-ounce can salmon
½ pound cottage cheese
½ cup sour cream
⅛ teaspoon salt

⅛ teaspoon Tabasco
1 tablespoon minced onions
½ teaspoon paprika

Drain and remove the skin and bones of the salmon. Combine in an electric blender bowl with all the remaining ingredients. Cover and blend until very smooth. Stop machine and stir down well once or twice. (Or beat ingredients until smooth.)

Makes about 2¼ cups.

LOMI LOMI (Hawaiian Salmon Spread)

1 pound smoked salmon
1 cup peeled chopped tomatoes

1 cup finely chopped green onions
¼ cup ice water

Soak the salmon in water to cover 3 hours; change the water twice. Drain; chop the salmon fine. Add the tomatoes and green onions, chop until a paste is formed, adding the water gradually. Chill. Heap in a deep bowl. Serve with toast or chips.

Makes about 2½ cups.

SMOKED SALMON SPREAD

1/3 cup heavy cream
¼ pound smoked salmon, shredded
½ teaspoon capers

⅛ teaspoon freshly ground black pepper

Put all the ingredients into the bowl of an electric blender and blend until smooth. Or chop the salmon and capers very fine, whip the cream and fold into the salmon with the pep-

20

per. Sprinkle top with a little pepper. Serve with sliced French bread or potato chips.

Makes about ¾ cup.

WHIPPED SMOKED SALMON SPREAD

¼ pound smoked salmon
¼ pound sweet butter
½ cup whipped cream

Chop the salmon to a paste. Cream the butter until fluffy and combine with the salmon. Fold in the whipped cream; pack into a mold and chill. Serve with thin slices of pumpernickel. Makes about 1½ cups.

BRANDADE DE MORUE (Fluffy Codfish Dip, Provencal)

1½ pounds salt cod
2 cloves garlic, minced
1 cup warm olive oil
1 cup warm light cream

2 tablespoons lemon juice
½ teaspoon white pepper
⅛ teaspoon nutmeg

Wash the codfish, cover with water and let soak overnight; change the water 3 times. Drain, cover with fresh water and bring to a boil; cook over low heat 30 minutes. Drain and discard the skin and bones; cut the fish in small pieces, then grind, chop or run in an electric blender with the garlic and 3 tablespoons oil until smooth. Gradually work in the remaining oil and then the cream, lemon juice, pepper and nutmeg. The mixture should be smooth and fluffy. Place over hot water and heat. Serve on toasted or sautéed French bread.

Makes about 2 cups.

CHOPPED HERRING

4 fillets of salt herring (2 herrings)
¼ cup chopped onions
½ cup chopped green pepper
3 hard-cooked egg yolks

3 tablespoons cider vinegar
2 slices white bread, trimmed
2 tablespoons vegetable oil

21

Soak the herring in water to cover 12 hours, changing the water twice. Drain.

Chop together the herring, onions, green pepper and egg yolks. Pour the vinegar over the bread and add to the herring with the oil. Chop until very smooth. Taste for seasoning, adding more vinegar if desired. Chill. Serve with toast squares or crisp crackers.

Makes about 3 cups.

HERRING AND VEGETABLE APPETIZER

3 fillets of salt herring	2 tablespoons vegetable oil
½ cup chopped tomatoes	½ teaspoon sugar
¼ cup chopped green onions	¼ teaspoon freshly ground black
½ cup chopped green pepper	pepper
2 tablespoons cider vinegar	

Cut the herring fillets into ¼-inch pieces. Toss with all the remaining ingredients. Chill 1 hour. Drain well, heap in a bowl and serve with thinly sliced rye bread.

Makes about 2 cups.

HERRING-CHEESE SPREAD

2 salt herring fillets	1 onion, chopped
2 cups milk	4 tablespoons grated apple
¼ pound butter	¼ pound cream cheese

Soak the herring in the milk overnight. Drain.

Melt 1 tablespoon butter in a skillet. Sauté the onion 10 minutes.

Grind the herring, onion and apple together in a food chopper. Cream the remaining butter and cream cheese together until smooth. Add the herring mixture, blending until very smooth. Pack into a crock and chill. Serve with black bread or crisp crackers.

Makes about 3½ cups.

KIPPERED HERRING SPREAD

1 can kippered herring
2 tablespoons grated onion
3 tablespoons mayonnaise

¼ cup finely chopped celery
1 hard-cooked egg yolk, mashed

Drain, skin and mash the kippers. Blend with the onions, mayonnaise, celery and egg yolk. Serve with crisp crackers or buttered toast rounds.

Makes about 1 cup.

CHICK PEA-ANCHOVY SPREAD, MEDITERRANEAN STYLE

1 16-ounce can chick peas
2 tablespoons olive oil
2 tablespoons minced onions
6 anchovies, finely chopped

2 tablespoons chopped parsley
¼ teaspoon freshly ground black pepper

Cook the undrained chick peas 10 minutes. Drain and purée in an electric blender with the oil, or mash very smooth. Cool. Mix in the onions, anchovies, parsley and pepper. Taste for seasoning and chill. Heap in a bowl. Serve with sesame crackers or thinly sliced Italian or French bread.

Makes about 2 cups.

LE SAUSSOON (Anchovy-Almond Spread, Provencal)

1 tablespoon chopped fresh mint
  or ½ teaspoon dried
8 anchovy fillets, minced
1 cup ground blanched almonds

½ cup olive oil
¼ cup water
⅛ teaspoon lemon juice

Chop, then pound together the mint and anchovies to a paste. Mix in a little of the almonds, a little oil, and then a little water and continue adding the ingredients until all are used up. Stir in the lemon juice. The resulting spread should look like a very thick mayonnaise. Serve with thinly sliced bread.

Makes about 1½ cups.

SAMBAL OEDANG (Indonesian Spiced Shrimp Spread)

¾ cup fine-grated packaged coconut
1 cup milk
½ cup chopped onions
2 garlic cloves, minced
1½ teaspoons salt
¾ teaspoon dried ground chili
  peppers

1 tablespoon lemon juice
2 teaspoons grated lemon rind
2 teaspoons brown sugar
1 teaspoon powdered ginger
3 tablespoons oil
1 pound raw shrimp, shelled,
  deveined, and chopped

Rinse the coconut under cold running water. Drain and combine with the milk in a saucepan. Bring to a boil, then let soak 1 hour. Drain, pressing out all the liquid. Reserve the liquid; discard the coconut.

Pound or chop to a paste the onions, garlic, salt, chili peppers, lemon juice, rind, brown sugar, and ginger. Heat the oil in a skillet; sauté the mixture 3 minutes, stirring frequently. Add the shrimp; cook over low heat, stirring steadily for 3 minutes. Blend in the coconut milk. Cook over low heat 10 minutes. Chill. Heap in a bowl and serve with crisp crackers.

Makes about 2½ cups.

SHRIMP DIP I

1 can frozen cream of shrimp soup
1 3-ounce package cream cheese
3 tablespoons chili sauce

½ teaspoon anchovy paste
⅛ teaspoon Tabasco

Thaw the frozen soup by placing can in hot water for 30 minutes. Beat the cheese until smooth, then with a rotary beater mix in the thawed soup, chili sauce, anchovy paste and Tabasco. Beat just until blended—overbeating will make mixture too thin. Makes about 1½ cups.

SHRIMP DIP II

½ pound cooked or canned shelled
  shrimp
½ pound cottage cheese
2 teaspoons grated onions

1 teaspoon lemon juice
½ teaspoon Worcestershire sauce
4 tablespoons sour cream

Finely chop the shrimp. Beat the cheese, onions, lemon juice, Worcestershire sauce and sour cream until smooth.

Mix in the shrimp. Correct seasoning. Serve with crisp raw vegetables or chips. Makes about 2 cups.

SHRIMP PASTE

1 pound cooked shrimp, shelled and deveined
½ teaspoon salt
Dash cayenne pepper
Dash nutmeg
Dash mace
6 tablespoons butter

Purée the shrimp until very smooth in an electric blender; or grind in a food chopper, then force through a sieve. Combine in a saucepan with the salt, cayenne pepper, nutmeg, mace and 3 tablespoons of the butter. Cook over low heat, stirring constantly until mixture boils. Taste for seasoning. Pack into a small mold or crock. Melt the remaining butter and pour over the top. Chill at least 4 hours. Serve with thinly sliced pumpernickel squares or crisp crackers. Makes about 1½ cups.

SHRIMP DUNKING SAUCE

1 cup chili sauce
3 tablespoons prepared horseradish
½ cup minced onions
¼ cup minced green pepper
2 tablespoons lemon juice
½ teaspoon freshly ground black pepper

Mix all the ingredients together; chill several hours before serving. Makes about 1¾ cups.

OREGON CLAM SPREAD

24 clams or 2 10½-ounce cans clams, minced
½ cup chopped onions
¾ cup diced tomatoes
½ cup chopped green pepper
2 tablespoons olive oil
2 tablespoons wine vinegar
⅛ teaspoon Tabasco

Chop the clams (drain canned clams) and combine with the onions, tomatoes, green pepper, oil, vinegar and Tabasco. Chill 3 hours. Drain and serve with toast squares.
Makes about 3 cups.

PISMO BEACH CLAM DIP

½ pound cream cheese
3 tablespoons sour cream
1 tablespoon grated onions

1½ teaspoons Worcestershire sauce
1 10½-ounce can minced clams,
   drained and chopped

Beat together until smooth the cream cheese, sour cream, onions and Worcestershire sauce. Mix in the clams. Turn into a bowl. Serve with potato chips, crisp raw vegetables or thinly sliced French bread.

Makes about 1 cup.

PIMIENTO-CLAM DIP

1 can frozen New England-style
   clam chowder
¼ pound cream cheese
1 7-ounce can minced clams, drained

3 tablespoons minced onions
¼ teaspoon Tabasco
3 tablespoons minced pimientos

Thaw the soup by placing can in hot water for 30 minutes. Beat the cream cheese until smooth, then with a rotary beater mix in the soup, clams, onions and Tabasco. Stir in the pimientos. Chill. If too thick, add a little heavy cream. Serve the dip in a bowl, surrounded with crisp raw vegetables or potato chips.

Makes about 2 cups.

CALIFORNIA CLAM-NUT SPREAD

1 3-ounce package cream cheese
1 10½-ounce can minced clams,
   drained and chopped

¼ cup ground almonds or
   Brazil nuts
½ teaspoon curry powder

Mash the cheese until smooth. Mix in the clams, then the nuts and curry powder. Serve with small squares of buttered toast or crisp crackers.

Makes about 1 cup.

CRAB-MEAT SPREAD

1 6½-ounce can crab meat
½ cup mayonnaise
1 tablespoon lemon juice
1 tablespoon dry sherry

⅛ teaspoon Tabasco
1 tablespoon instant minced
   green onions

Drain the crab meat, then carefully discard the cartilage. Put the crab meat in an electric blender bowl with all the remaining ingredients. Cover and blend until very smooth. Stop machine and stir down well once. (Or chop ingredients to a paste.) Serve on crisp crackers or toast.

Makes about 1¼ cups.

CURRIED CRAB-MEAT SPREAD

½ pound crab meat
¼ cup mayonnaise
2 tablespoons sour cream

1 tablespoon grated onions
1 tablespoon minced parsley
1 tablespoon curry powder

Pick over the crab meat, discarding any cartilage. Chop the crab meat. Blend together with all the remaining ingredients. Taste for seasoning. Heap in a bowl and serve with thin buttered toast or crisp crackers.

Makes about 2 cups.

INDIAN CRAB-MEAT HORS D'OEUVRE

1 pound crab meat
3 tablespoons butter
1 cup chopped onions
¾ teaspoon salt
½ teaspoon freshly ground black pepper

½ teaspoon powdered fennel
¾ teaspoon turmeric
1 clove garlic, minced
1 tablespoon lemon juice

Pick over and finely chop the crab meat, discarding any cartilage.

Melt the butter in a skillet; sauté the onions 5 minutes, stirring frequently. Add the salt, pepper, fennel, turmeric, garlic and lemon juice. Cook over low heat 5 minutes, stirring frequently. Serve in small shells or heap on rounds of toast.

Makes about 2 cups.

CRAB RAVIGOTE, NEW ORLEANS FASHION

¼ cup tarragon vinegar
1 pound cooked or canned crab meat, flaked
2 tablespoons chopped chives or green onions
3 tablespoons chopped pimiento

1 teaspoon salt
½ teaspoon freshly ground black pepper
½ cup mayonnaise
2 tablespoons chopped capers

Pour the vinegar over the flaked crab meat and chill for 15 minutes. Drain the crab meat, pressing gently to remove the excess vinegar. Combine in a bowl with the chopped chives or onions, pimiento, salt, pepper and mayonnaise and mix together lightly. Heap in a serving dish and sprinkle with the capers. Serve with crisp crackers or toast squares.

Makes about 2 cups.

CHICKEN SPREAD

¼ cup mayonnaise
2 tablespoons sour cream
1½ cups chopped cooked chicken
¼ teaspoon salt

¼ teaspoon freshly ground black pepper
1 tablespoon grated onions
4 slices crisp bacon, finely crumbled

Stir together the mayonnaise and sour cream. Toss the chicken with the salt, pepper, onions and bacon, then fold in the mayonnaise mixture. Heap in a bowl. Serve with tiny split hot biscuits or buttered toast fingers.

Makes about 1¾ cups.

CURRIED CHICKEN SPREAD, INDIAN STYLE

¾ cup mayonnaise
2 5-ounce cans boned chicken
½ cup flaked coconut

½ teaspoon salt
2½ teaspoons curry powder
1 tablespoon minced onions

Combine all the ingredients in the bowl of an electric blender. Blend until very smooth. Stop machine and stir down well once or twice (or chop ingredients to a smooth paste). Serve on thin bread or crisp crackers.

Makes about 2 cups.

SALPICON À LA REINE
(Chicken-Mushroom Spread, French Style)

2 tablespoons butter
¼ pound mushrooms, chopped
1½ cups ground cooked chicken or turkey
1/3 cup ground blanched almonds

1 teaspoon salt
¼ teaspoon freshly ground black pepper
¼ cup mayonnaise

Melt the butter in a skillet; sauté the mushrooms 5 minutes. Cool, then combine with the chicken, almonds, salt, pepper and mayonnaise. Blend well and taste for seasoning. Heap in a bowl, or make canapés.

Makes about 2 cups.

HAM DIP

1½ cups ground cooked ham
4 tablespoons mayonnaise
4 tablespoons sour cream

1 tablespoon prepared mustard
2 teaspoons prepared horseradish
2 tablespoons ketchup

Mix all the ingredients together until smooth. If mixture is too thick for a dip, add a little more sour cream. Chill. Serve with potato chips or crisp vegetables.

Makes about 2 cups.

DEVILED HAM-CHEESE SPREAD

1 cup (¼ pound) grated cheddar cheese
2 2¼-ounce cans deviled ham
2 teaspoons prepared mustard

Mix all the ingredients together until smooth. Serve with toast fingers or crisp crackers. The spread may also be heaped on toast, then placed in a 425° oven for 5 minutes. Serve hot.

Makes about 1½ cups.

ENGLISH DEVILED HAM SPREAD

1 4½-ounce can deviled ham
1 3-ounce package cream cheese
1 tablespoon minced onions

2 teaspoons tomato paste
⅛ teaspoon Tabasco
2 tablespoons parsley

Combine all the ingredients in a bowl of an electric blender. Cover and blend until very smooth. Stop machine and stir down once (or beat all the ingredients until very smooth).

Makes about 1 cup.

TONGUE SPREAD

½ pound cooked tongue
½ cup chopped black olives
1/3 cup mayonnaise

½ cup ground almonds or
Brazil nuts

Grind or chop the tongue and blend with the remaining ingredients. Taste for seasoning. Heap in a bowl and serve with thinly sliced pumpernickel. Makes about 2½ cups.

CHIPPED BEEF DIP

¼ pound chipped beef
1 clove garlic
2 cups (½ pound) grated Swiss cheese

1/3 cup dry white wine
¼ teaspoon freshly ground black pepper

Grind the beef in a food chopper, or chop very fine. Rub a chafing dish or top of a double boiler with the garlic. Add the cheese and wine; place over hot water until cheese melts, stirring frequently. Mix in the pepper and beef. Taste for seasoning. Serve in a chafing dish to keep hot, and surround with cubes of French bread for dipping.

Makes about 2 cups.

CHUTNEY DIP

½ pound cream cheese
2 tablespoons heavy cream

1 tablespoon curry powder
¾ cup chopped chutney

Beat the cheese and cream until smooth. Add curry powder and chutney, beating well. Place in a small mold. Chill overnight. Unmold and serve with potato chips.

Makes about 1¼ cups.

30

INDIAN DIP

2 green onions, chopped
¾ cup diced cucumber
½ cup diced green pepper
½ cup sliced celery
½ teaspoon salt

½ teaspoon chili powder
1 teaspoon turmeric
¼ teaspoon powdered ginger
1 tablespoon tomato paste
1 cup sour cream

Purée all the vegetables in an electric blender or chop very fine. Drain all the liquid thoroughly. Mix the puréed vegetables with the salt, chili powder, turmeric, ginger and tomato paste, then blend into the sour cream. Chill. Serve as a dip with crisp raw vegetables, potato chips or cubes of cheese.
Makes about 1½ cups.

HORSERADISH DIP

2 3-ounce packages cream cheese
¼ cup sour cream
3 tablespoons freshly grated
  horseradish or ¼ cup prepared,
  well drained
½ teaspoon salt

¼ teaspoon freshly ground black
  pepper
½ teaspoon paprika
2 tablespoons chopped dill or
  parsley

Beat the cheese, gradually beating in the sour cream, then the horseradish, salt, pepper and paprika. Turn into a bowl, chill and sprinkle with the dill or parsley. Serve surrounded with crisp raw vegetables.
Makes about 1 cup.

MASLINE FRECATE (Rumanian Olive Spread)

½ pound ripe olives (Italian or
  Greek)
½ pound (2 sticks) soft butter
⅛ teaspoon freshly ground black
  pepper

⅛ teaspoon ground fennel seeds
2 tablespoons minced chives or
  green onions
2 tablespoons minced parsley

Pit the olives and purée in an electric blender or chop very fine. Cream the butter; beat in the pepper, fennel, chives, parsley and olives until well blended. Chill. Serve on or with pumpernickel.
Makes about 1¼ cups.

OLIVE DIP, YUGOSLAVIAN STYLE

¼ pound cream cheese	2 teaspoons minced onions
¾ cup sour cream	½ teaspoon paprika
2 tablespoons lemon juice	1 cup sliced green or black olives

Break the cream cheese into small pieces and put in the
bowl of an electric blender. Add the sour cream, lemon
juice, onions and paprika. Cover and blend until very smooth.
Remove cover and add ¼ cup olives at a time. Stop machine and stir down once or twice. (Or beat cheese with sour
cream and seasonings until smooth, then mix in finely
chopped olives.)

Makes about 1½ cups.

FRIJOLES PARA SOPEAR (Mexican Chili-Bean Dip)

1 10½-ounce can condensed black bean soup	1 clove garlic, minced
¼ cup minced onions	2 teaspoons chili powder

Blend all the ingredients together. Chill. Serve with corn
chips or potato chips.

Makes about 1¼ cups.

FOOL MUDAMMAS (Arabic Bean Appetizer)

2 cups dried white beans	½ teaspoon freshly ground black pepper
3 teaspoons salt	¼ cup finely chopped chives or green onions
½ cup sesame or olive oil	
2 cloves garlic, minced	
¼ cup lemon juice	

Wash the beans, cover with water and bring to a boil. Let
soak 1 hour. Drain, add fresh water to cover. Bring to a
boil and cook over low heat 2 hours, or until bean skins
burst, adding the salt after 1 hour of cooking time. Drain,
mash and put in a bowl.

Beat together the oil, garlic, lemon juice and pepper. Mix
into the beans. Chill. Sprinkle with the chives or green
onions. Serve with thinly sliced bread, crisp crackers or
Arabian bread.

Makes about 3 cups.

AVOCADO-CHEESE DIP

¼ pound Roquefort or blue cheese
3 tablespoons olive oil
2 avocados
2 tablespoons lemon juice
½ teaspoon salt
¼ teaspoon freshly ground black
   pepper

Mash the cheese very smooth, then beat in the olive oil. Peel and mash the avocados. Immediately add to the cheese with the lemon juice, salt and pepper, stirring until smooth. Taste for seasoning. Or combine all the ingredients in a blender and blend until smooth. Heap in a bowl and serve with potato chips.

Makes about 2 cups.

AVOCADO-CREAM CHEESE SPREAD

1 avocado
¼ pound cream cheese
1 clove garlic, minced
2 tablespoons lemon juice
¼ teaspoon freshly ground black
   pepper

Remove the pulp of the avocado and mash smooth. Beat the cheese until soft and smooth; combine with the avocado, garlic, lemon juice and pepper. Serve in a bowl with crackers or toast fingers.

Makes about 1 cup.

CREAMED AVOCADO DIP, CALIFORNIA STYLE

½ cup heavy cream
½ cup chili sauce
2 tablespoons minced onions
1 tablespoon lime or lemon juice
1 teaspoon salt
Dash Tabasco
1 teaspoon Worcestershire sauce
3 avocados

Mix together the cream, chili sauce, onions, lime juice, salt, Tabasco and Worcestershire sauces. Peel and mash the avocados. Mix into the dressing. Serve in a bowl surrounded with chips, toast fingers or crisp vegetables.

Makes about 3 cups.

GUACAMOLE (Mexican Avocado Dip)

1 large ripe avocado
1 tomato, peeled and chopped fine
3 tablespoons grated onions
1 teaspoon salt

¼ teaspoon freshly ground black pepper
1½ teaspoons chili powder
2 teaspoons cider vinegar

Cut the avocado in half lengthwise. Scoop out the pulp and mash. Immediately mix in the tomato, onions, salt, pepper, chili powder and vinegar. Taste for seasoning. Serve with corn or potato chips.

Makes about 1¼ cups.

CALIFORNIA AVOCADO-OLIVE DIP

1 large ripe avocado
2 tablespoons lemon juice
2 tablespoons mayonnaise
2 tablespoons minced onions

½ teaspoon salt
⅛ teaspoon Tabasco
½ cup chopped black or green olives

Cut the avocado in half and scoop out the pulp. Mash very smooth; blend in the lemon juice, mayonnaise, onions, salt and Tabasco. Stir in the olives. Serve with shrimp, crisp vegetables or crisp crackers.

Makes about 1 cup.

PICANTE DE AGUACATES (Avocado-Egg Dip, Venezuelan Style)

3 avocados
6 hard-cooked egg yolks
2 canned *chiles jalapeños*, or ½ teaspoon dried ground red peppers

¼ cup finely chopped onions
3 tablespoons minced parsley
3 tablespoons lemon juice
1½ teaspoons salt

Peel the avocados and chop fine with the egg yolks, red peppers, onions and parsley. Mix in the lemon juice and salt. Taste for seasoning. Serve in a bowl as a dip with chips, toast or shrimp.

Makes about 3 cups.

GEHOCKTE EIER (Chopped Eggs and Onions, Jewish Style)

1 medium onion
6 hard-cooked eggs
1 teaspoon salt

¼ teaspoon white pepper
3 tablespoons rendered chicken fat or melted butter

Chop the onion until very fine. Add the eggs and continue chopping. Mix in the salt, pepper and fat. Chill. Serve with sesame crackers or toast squares.

Makes about 1¼ cups.

BAGNA CAUDA (Hot Italian Anchovy Dip)

¼ pound butter
¼ cup olive oil
5 cloves garlic, thinly sliced

½ cup finely chopped anchovies
Crisp raw vegetables

Combine the butter, oil and garlic in a small saucepan. Place over very low heat or boiling water for 15 minutes, but do not let the mixture boil. Mix in the anchovies until dissolved. Pour into a small chafing dish or a candle warmer to keep warm. Surround with any crisp raw vegetables.

Makes about ¾ cup.

PATLAGELE VINETE TOCATA
(Rumanian Eggplant Spread)

1 large eggplant
½ cup olive oil
3 tablespoons lemon juice
1 teaspoon salt

¼ teaspoon freshly ground black pepper
Finely chopped onions
Ripe black olives

Wash the eggplant and wrap loosely in foil. Bake in a 400° oven 45 minutes. Unwrap the foil and place eggplant under the broiler until skin is black on all sides. Remove from broiler and let stand until cool enough to handle. Wet the fingers with cold water and peel off the skin.

Place on a chopping board and chop very fine, adding 1 tablespoon of the oil as you chop. Transfer to a wooden bowl; with a wooden spoon beat in the remaining oil drop by drop alternately with the lemon juice. Mix in the salt and pepper and continue beating with the wooden spoon until the seeds disappear and paste is firm. Taste for seasoning and chill.

Just before serving, heap the paste in a serving dish and put the onions on one side and the olives on the other. Serve with thin slices of buttered black bread.

Makes about 3 cups.

BABA GHANNOUJ (Arabian Eggplant Appetizer)

2 2-pound eggplants	1½ teaspoons salt
½ cup sesame seed or vegetable oil	Cayenne pepper
1/3 cup lemon juice	¼ cup chopped parsley
1 clove garlic, minced fine	

Wash and dry the eggplants. Line a broiler pan with aluminum foil and place the eggplants on it. Broil close to the source of heat until the skins are black and eggplants tender. Remove, cool slightly and peel.

Beat the oil, lemon juice, garlic and salt until thick. Mash the eggplant, then beat smooth with an electric mixer or whisk. Gradually beat in the oil mixture. Heap in a bowl and chill. Sprinkle with a dash of cayenne pepper and the parsley. Serve as a dip with crisp crackers, Arabian bread or romaine lettuce leaves.

Makes about 4 cups.

TARATA (Greek Eggplant Spread)

2 1½-pound eggplants	1½ teaspoons salt
4 tablespoons olive oil	½ teaspoon freshly ground black
¾ cup sliced onions	pepper
1 cup sliced green pepper	½ cup yogurt
2 cloves garlic, minced	

Peel the eggplant; sauté in the olive oil with the onions, green pepper and garlic until soft, do not let brown. Stir in the salt and pepper, then chop. Cool, then mix in the yogurt. Serve very cold with thinly sliced black bread.

Makes about 3 cups.

EGGPLANT CAVIAR, RUSSIAN STYLE

1 2-pound eggplant
½ cup chopped onions
1 cup peeled chopped tomatoes
1 slice white bread, trimmed
3 tablespoons cider vinegar

¼ cup vegetable oil
1½ teaspoons salt
½ teaspoon freshly ground black pepper
½ teaspoon sugar

Wash the eggplant and wrap in aluminum foil. Bake in a 375° oven 1 hour, opening the foil for the last 15 minutes. Let stand until cool enough to handle, then peel.

Chop together the eggplant, onions, tomatoes and the bread soaked in the vinegar. Mix in the oil, salt, pepper and sugar. Continue chopping until smooth. Chill. Serve with thin pumpernickel or crackers.

Makes about 4 cups.

MELITZANES SALATA (Greek Chopped Eggplant Appetizer)

1 2-pound eggplant
¼ cup minced onions
2 tablespoons vegetable or olive oil
4 tablespoons lemon juice

1½ teaspoons salt
¼ teaspoon pepper
1 teaspoon sugar

Wash the eggplant, dry and wrap loosely in aluminum foil. Bake in a 475° oven 1 hour. Cool and peel.

Chop the eggplant very smooth. Beat in the onions, oil, lemon juice, salt, pepper and sugar. Chill. Serve with thinly sliced pumpernickel and black olives.

Makes about 4 cups.

CAPONATA ALLA SICILIANA (Sicilian Eggplant Antipasto)

2 1½-pound eggplants
2 teaspoons salt
½ cup olive oil
1½ pounds tomatoes, diced
2 stalks celery, diced
½ cup sliced black olives

2 tablespoons capers
1 tablespoon vinegar
1 teaspoon sugar
½ teaspoon freshly ground black pepper

Peel and dice the eggplants and sprinkle with 1 teaspoon salt; let stand 10 minutes. Drain. Heat half the oil in a skillet; brown the eggplant in it.

In a saucepan, heat the remaining oil, mix in the tomatoes and celery; cook over low heat 15 minutes. Add the olives, capers, vinegar, sugar, remaining salt, and pepper; cook 15 minutes. Add the browned eggplant and cook 15 minutes longer. Taste for seasoning; chill. Garnish with additional capers and olives, if desired. Serve with Italian bread.

Makes about 4 cups.

FONDUE JURASSIENNE (Hot Cheese Dip, Swiss Style)

2 cloves garlic, sliced
1½ cups dry white wine
3 cups (¾ pound) Gruyère cheese
1/3 cup milk
½ teaspoon salt
¼ teaspoon freshly ground white pepper

1½ tablespoons kirsch (cherry liqueur)
2 tablespoons sweet butter
French bread or toast

Put the garlic and wine in an earthenware casserole and cook over medium heat 10 minutes. Strain wine and reserve.

Combine the cheese and milk in the casserole and cook over low heat, stirring constantly, until cheese is melted and mixture smooth and creamy. Stir in the salt, pepper, kirsch and wine, then the butter. Serve at once with pieces of crusty French bread or toast on forks or skewers for dunking.

Makes about 3 cups.

KOROZOTT LIPTÓI (Hungarian Cheese Spread)

¼ pound butter
½ pound cream cheese (or Hungarian liptói cheese, if available)
1 teaspoon caraway seeds

¾ teaspoon sweet paprika
2 teaspoons chopped chives, green onions or grated onions
1 teaspoon chopped capers

Cream together the butter and cheese. Blend in the caraway seeds, paprika, chives and capers. Serve with thinly sliced pumpernickel.

Makes about 1½ cups.

SACHERKÄSE (Viennese Cheese Appetizer)

½ pound cottage cheese
2 hard-cooked egg yolks
3 tablespoons soft butter
1 tablespoon minced onions

4 anchovy fillets
1 teaspoon prepared mustard
1 teaspoon olive oil
⅛ teaspoon paprika

Combine all the ingredients in an electric blender and blend until smooth, or force through a sieve. Heap in a bowl, and garnish with additional anchovy fillets, sliced hard-cooked eggs and parsley sprigs, if desired. Serve with thinly sliced pumpernickel or rye bread.

Makes about 2 cups.

SHERRIED CHEESE SPREAD

1 cup (¼ pound) grated cheddar
  cheese
¾ cup sour cream

¼ cup dry sherry
Dash cayenne pepper

Beat all the ingredients together until smooth and fluffy. Chill. Serve with small squares of pumpernickel, buttered toast or crisp crackers.

Makes about 1½ cups.

COGNAC-CHEESE SPREAD

¼ pound Roquefort, Gorgonzola or blue cheese
1 3-ounce package cream cheese
1/3 cup cognac

Mash the cheeses until smooth. Beat in the cognac. Serve with crackers.

Makes about ¾ cup.

CARAWAY CHEESE SPREAD

2 3-ounce packages cream cheese
¼ cup sour cream
1 tablespoon grated onions

¼ cup caraway seeds
2 tablespoons drained chopped
  capers

Beat the cream cheese and sour cream until smooth and fluffy. Mix in the onions, caraway seeds and capers. Serve on small rounds or squares of pumpernickel or rye bread.

Makes about 1 cup.

MIXED CHEESE SPREAD

¼ pound Liederkranz cheese	1 3-ounce package cream cheese
2 cups (½ pound) grated cheddar cheese	4 tablespoons butter
	½ cup dry white wine
¼ pound blue cheese	Dash cayenne pepper

Remove the rind of the Liederkranz cheese and combine with all the remaining ingredients in the top of a double boiler. Place over hot water and cook, stirring frequently until cheeses are melted and smooth. Pour into a jug or mold and chill until firm. Serve with crisp crackers or thinly sliced bread.

Makes about 3 cups.

CANAPÉS

CANAPÉS, the small open French sandwiches, are probably of Russian origin and were one of the chief features of their zakuska. The Norwegians and Swedes have a larger version called smorbrod, and the Danes call it smorrebrod, eaten not only as appetizers, but sometimes as luncheon or late evening snacks. But they all bear a resemblance. Pieces of bread or toast are cut in various shapes—squares, diamonds, rounds, rectangles—which are then spread with a plain or flavored butter and tastefully garnished. Small pastry rounds or squares, crisp crackers or brioches may also be used as a base for canapés.

The variety is endless, but flavor and eye appeal are both important. Use ingredients to tempt the appetite, and decorate tastefully. Many canapés may be glazed with aspic, which offers a protective coating, keeping the food underneath from drying out. When preparing canapés, remember to keep them small and to vary the shape as well as the ingredients.

Equipment can be a great help in preparing attractive canapés. Sharp knives are essential, so foods can be cut very thin. An electric blender is wonderful for making pastes and spreads. A set of canapé cutters in various shapes is also of great use. The French-type grater is also a necessity, particularly for eggs, as it provides a fluffy grated egg. Of course a pastry bag with different-shaped tubes is necessary for the final professional garnish. Use your taste and imagination for an eye-appealing presentation, and always arrange the canapés in an attractive manner on china or silver that will serve as the proper background.

There are two very unusual canapés in this section. On the French Riviera, the culinary style calls for the use of garlic and olive oil in many dishes, and the anchoïade, prepared with chopped anchovies, is spicy and delicious, ideal with drinks. In Germany they prepare Schlemmerschnitte, with raw ground beef and caviar—an apparently odd matching of ingredients, but one that has a tantalizing taste.

SAUTÉED BREAD FOR CANAPÉS

Use white bread, sliced ¼ inch thick. Cut into 1½—2-inch rounds or squares. Melt enough butter in a skillet so that it is ⅛ inch in depth. Sauté the bread until delicately browned on both sides. Add butter as needed.

FRENCH CANAPÉ BUTTERS

Canapé butters are used in place of plain butter, and may also be used for decorating the canapés.

Use ¼ pound (1 stick) softened butter. Cream it smooth, then blend in one of the following combinations:

Anchovy:
    3 tablespoons anchovy paste

Cheese:
    2 tablespoons grated Parmesan or other cheese

Chivry:
1 tablespoon each of finely minced herbs

Deviled:
2 tablespoons minced chives, 1 teaspoon Tabasco, 2 tablespoons Worcestershire sauce, and 2 teaspoons dry mustard

Garlic:
I tablespoon crushed garlic and ½ teaspoon salt

Horseradish:
3 tablespoons finely grated fresh horshradish

Lobster:
¼ cup minced cooked lobster meat or lobster coral. Force through a sieve after it is blended with the butter.

Mustard:
1 tablespoon prepared mustard

Paprika:
4 teaspoons paprika, ½ teaspoon salt and 1 tablespoon finely grated onion

Parsley:
¼ cup finely chopped parsley and ½ teaspoon salt

Roquefort:
¼ pound butter, ¼ pound Roquefort cheese, and 3 tablespoons ground nuts

Shrimp:

½ pound cooked cleaned shrimp chopped to a paste and ½ teaspoon salt

Smoked Salmon:

1 slice smoked salmon, chopped to a fine paste

Watercress:

⅓ cup finely chopped watercress and 1 tablespoon anchovy butter

ASPIC-COATED CANAPÉS

Use thinly sliced trimmed bread, spread with butter or a canapé butter, then put over it a thin slice of smoked salmon, sturgeon, turkey, chicken, tongue, ham or roast beef cut to fit. Brush the surface with aspic and chill until set. Cut each slice into fancy shapes, squares or triangles. Decorate the tops with truffles, olives, pimientos, etc. and brush with aspic again. Chill until set.

ASPICS FOR GLAZING

All aspics are prepared in the same manner.

Chicken Aspic:

2 envelopes (tablespoons) gelatin
2 cups chicken broth
2 tablespoons dry white wine
¼ teaspoon white pepper
1 eggs white, stiffly beaten
Crushed eggshells

Tomato Aspic:

2 envelopes (tablespoons) gelatin
1½ cups tomato juice
½ cup chicken broth
½ teaspoon salt
¼ teaspoon white pepper
½ teaspoon sugar
1 egg white, stiffly beaten
Crushed eggshells

Port Wine Aspic:

2 envelopes (tablespoons) gelatin	¼ teaspoon white pepper
1 cup Port wine	1 egg white, stiffly beaten
1 cup chicken broth	Crushed eggshells

Combine all the ingredients in a saucepan. Cook over low heat, stirring steadily until mixture comes to a rolling boil. Remove from the heat and let stand 10 minutes. Strain through a sieve lined with fine cheesecloth. Taste for seasoning and cool. A drop of food coloring may be added if you prefer a tinted aspic.

When the aspic begins to set, brush it heavily onto the selected ingredient, then chill until firm. To make decorative cutouts, pour the aspic into a dish to a depth of ¼ inch. Chill until very firm, then cut into fancy shapes.

RIBBON CANAPÉS

Use 6 very thin slices of white bread for each pile. Trim the bread, then spread with any spread or filling. Stack the spread slices, leaving the top slice plain. Press all together gently, wrap in foil or Saran wrap and chill. Cut into ¼-inch slices, then cut each slice in half on the diagonal.

Makes about 32.

HOT SEAFOOD CANAPÉS

1½ cups cooked shrimp, lobster or crab meat	3 tablespoons dry sherry
	Dash cayenne pepper
3 tablespoons butter	½ teaspoon A.1. Sauce
½ cup grated Parmesan cheese	Round crackers or toast rounds
1 egg yolk	

Chop the seafood very fine. Cream the butter and cheese together; blend in the egg yolk, sherry, cayenne and A.1. Sauce. Mix in the seafood. Put a heaping teaspoon of the mixture on each cracker or toast round; place on a baking sheet. Bake in a preheated 425° oven 5 minutes. Serve hot. Makes about 48.

MIXED SEAFOOD CANAPÉS

12 shucked oysters	2 egg yolks
6 tablespoons butter	½ pound shrimp, cooked, cleaned
½ cup chopped green onions	and diced
¼ cup chopped green pepper	½ pound crab meat
5 tablesoons flour	8 slices toast, trimmed and
½ cup dry white wine	quartered
2 cups bottled clam juice	3 tablespoons dry bread crumbs
⅛ teaspoon Tabasco	8 anchovy fillets, cut in 4 pieces

Cover the oysters with water, bring to a boil, drain and chop coarsely.

Melt 4 tablespoons butter in a saucepan; sauté the onions and pepper 5 minutes. Blend in the flour. Gradually add the wine and clam juice, stirring steadily to the boiling point, then stir in the Tabasco. Cook over low heat 5 minutes.

Beat the egg yolks in a bowl; gradually add the hot mixture, stirring steadily to prevent curdling. Return to saucepan and cook, stirring steadily until thickened, but do not let boil. Remove from heat and mix in the shrimp, crab meat and oysters. Taste for seasoning.

Spread the seafood mixture on the toast. Sprinkle with the bread crumbs, place an anchovy piece on each, dot with the remaining butter and bake in a 375° oven 5 minutes or until bubbly hot and delicately browned. Serve hot. Makes 32.

CANAPÉS AUX ANCHOIS (French Anchovy Canapes)

18 2-inch rounds of toast	18 rolled anchovies
Anchovy butter (see recipe)	½ cup minced parsley

Spread the toast rounds with anchovy butter and place a rolled anchovy in the center. Coat the edges with parsley. Makes 18.

CURRIED ANCHOVY CANAPÉS

2 cans anchovy fillets	1 tablespoon curry powder
4 tablespoons soft butter	6 slices toast
4 tablespoons cream cheese	Minced parsley

Drain the anchovies and chop fine. Beat the butter, cream cheese and curry powder until smooth. Mix in the anchovies. Trim the toast and cut each slice into 4 strips or squares. Spread with the anchovy mixture. Sprinkle with the parsley.
Makes 24.

PIMIENTO-ANCHOVY CANAPÉS

Marinate pimientos in a little oil, garlic and chopped parsley for 30 minutes. Drain. Cut the pimientos to fit rounds or squares of toast, and arrange anchovy fillets on top in a criss-cross design.

ANCHOÏADE (Anchovy Canapes, Riviera Style)

1 can anchovy fillets	2 tablespoons olive oil
3 cloves garlic, chopped	¼ teaspoon wine vinegar
2 tablespoons bread crumbs	10 slices French bread, lightly
¼ teaspoon freshly ground black pepper	toasted

Pound the undrained anchovy fillets and garlic in a mortar, or chop very fine. Add the bread crumbs and pepper; mix to a smooth paste and add the oil and wine vinegar. Brush the bread with olive oil, spread thinly with the anchovy mixture and broil 3 minutes. Serve very hot.
Makes 10.

STURGEON CANAPÉS

12 slices smoked sturgeon	½ teaspoon anchovy paste
Aspic (see recipe)	Dash cayenne pepper
1 truffle, cut into 12 slivers or stars	12 2-inch bread rounds
4 tablespoons soft butter	¾ cup finely chopped green pepper

Trim brown edges off the sturgeon and cut 2-inch pieces out of the center. Roll up the 2-inch pieces and fasten with toothpicks. Brush with aspic, put a piece of truffle on each and chill. Chop the remaining pieces of sturgeon.

Cream the butter; blend in the anchovy paste, cayenne pepper and chopped sturgeon. Spread the bread rounds with the mixture. Place a sturgeon roll in the center of each, and decorate the edges with the green pepper. Makes 12.

CANAPÉS AUX CREVETTES (Shrimp-Dill Canapes)

2 pounds shrimp, cooked, shelled and deveined
Buttered toast rounds
¼ cup minced dill
¾ cup mayonnaise
¼ teaspoon freshly ground black pepper

Cut each shrimp in half lengthwise. Arrange 3 halves on a toast round. Mix the dill, mayonnaise and pepper. Put through a pastry tube with a star or rose top, onto the shrimp, or put a dab on with a spoon. Garnish the tray with lemon wedges and sprigs of dill. Makes about 24.

CRAB-MEAT CANAPÉS AU GRATIN

½ pound crab meat
3 tablespoons butter
1 tablespoon minced onions
3 tablespoons flour
¾ cup light cream
¼ cup dry vermouth
¾ teaspoon salt
Dash cayenne pepper
½ cup grated Parmesan cheese
Toast

Pick over the crab meat, discarding any cartilage. Melt the butter in a saucepan; sauté the onions 2 minutes. Blend in the flour until smooth. Add the cream and wine, stirring steadily to the boiling point, then cook over low heat 5 minutes. Mix in the salt, cayenne pepper and crab meat. Taste for seasoning.

Cut the toast in small rounds, using a 2-inch cutter. Heap the crab-meat mixture on them. Sprinkle with Parmesan cheese and bake in a 425° oven, on the upper level, 5 minutes, or until browned. Makes about 48.

CRAB ASPIC CANAPÉS

½ pound crab meat
2 envelopes (tablespoons) gelatin
½ cup dry vermouth
1 cup mayonnaise
1 teaspoon lemon juice
2 tablespoons ketchup

1 tablespoon grated onions
½ teaspoon salt
Dash cayenne pepper
1 tablespoon minced parsley
½ cup heavy cream, whipped

Pick over the crab meat, discarding any cartilage; flake. Soften the gelatin in the vermouth, then place over hot water, stirring until dissolved. Cool. Mix together the gelatin, mayannaise, lemon juice, ketchup, onions, salt, cayenne and parsley. Fold in the whipped cream. Chill until mixture just begins to set. Fold in the crab meat.

Lightly oil 4 juice glasses (about 4 ounces each). Pour the mixture into them. Chill until very firm. Unmold carefully; cut into ¼-inch slices with a very sharp cold knife. Place on a toast round or cracker. Makes about 48.

HOT CRAB-MEAT CANAPÉS

1 7½-ounce can crab meat
1 tablespoon minced onions
¼ cup piccalilli

3 tablespoons mayonnaise
6 slices toast, trimmed and cut in half

Pick over the crab meat, discarding any cartilage; flake fine. Mix in the onions, piccalilli and mayonnaise. Spread on the toast. Put under a hot broiler until delicately browned. Makes 12 canapés.

CLAM CANAPÉS

¼ pound cream cheese
1 10½-ounce can minced clams, drained and chopped
½ teaspoon Worcestershire sauce

2 tablespoons grated onions
1 egg white, stiffly beaten
24 1-inch toasted bread rounds

Beat the cheese until smooth. Blend in the clams, Worcestershire sauce and onions. Fold in the egg white. Heap on the bread rounds. Arrange on a cooky sheet. Bake in a 400°

oven 5 minutes or until puffed and browned. Serve immediately.
Makes 24.

CLAM AND CHEDDAR CHEESE CANAPÉS

1 cup (¼ pound) grated cheddar cheese	2 tablespoons chopped parsley
	1 tablespoon grated onions
1 8-ounce can minced clams, drained	Toast rounds
Dash cayenne pepper	

Mix together all the ingredients but the toast. Spread on
toast rounds and broil until delicately browned.
Makes about 16 canapés.

SAUTÉED OYSTER CANAPÉS

12 shucked oysters	1 teaspoon Worcestershire sauce
4 tablespoons butter	2 tablespoons lemon juice
1 tablespoon minced onions	12 toast rounds

Drain and dry the oysters. Melt the butter in a skillet. Mix
in the onions, Worcestershire sauce and lemon juice and add
the oysters. Cook over low heat until edges of oysters curl,
basting and turning the oysters several times. Put an oyster
on each toast round.
Makes 12.

Variation: Sautéed Clam Canapés

Add 1 clove minced garlic to the butter and substitute
clams for oysters.

CANAPÉS DE SARDINES (Hot Sardine Canapes)

2 cans skinless boneless sardines	¼ teaspoon freshly ground black pepper
½ cup grated cheddar cheese	
Dash Tabasco	Buttered toast squares

Drain and mash the sardines. Mix with the cheese, Tabasco
and pepper. Heap on the toast squares, arrange on a baking
pan and bake in a 350° oven 10 minutes.
Makes about 24.

DEVILED SARDINE CANAPÉS

2 cans sardines
4 tablespoons prepared mustard
2 tablespoons lemon juice

½ cup soft bread crumbs
Buttered toast fingers

Drain the oil of the sardines and combine oil with the mustard and lemon juice. Dip each sardine in the mixture, then in the bread crumbs. Arrange on a greased baking pan and broil until delicately browned on both sides.

Have the toast fingers the same size as the sardines. Put a sardine on each finger and secure with a toothpick. Serve hot, garnished with lemon wedges.

Makes about 20.

CANAPÉS MARGUERY

2 7¾-ounce cans tuna fish
1 can anchovies
½ cup chopped green pepper
2 tablespoons chopped pimientos

3 hard-cooked egg yolks, chopped
½ cup mayonnaise
½ cup chili sauce
Dash Tabasco

Drain the tuna fish and chop with the undrained anchovies. Add the green pepper, pimientos and egg yolks. Chop to a paste. Heap on 2-inch rounds of sautéed bread. Mix together the mayonnaise, chili sauce and Tabasco; cover the tuna mixture. Place under the broiler for 2 minutes and serve hot.

Makes about 20.

CANAPÉ LORENZO

2 tomatoes, peeled and chopped
2 hard-cooked eggs
2 green peppers, chopped
2 anchovy fillets
4 sardines
¼ cup tuna fish
1 teaspoon salt

¼ teaspoon freshly ground black
   pepper
6 slices white bread, trimmed and
   cut in triangles
4 tablespoons butter
½ cup Russian dressing
Worcestershire sauce

Drain the tomatoes very well and mix with the eggs, green peppers, anchovies, sardines, tuna fish, salt and pepper until very smooth. Heat in a double boiler. Sauté the bread in the

butter until lightly browned on both sides. Heap the mixture on the toast and spread with Russian dressing. Sprinkle with a few drops of Worcestershire sauce and serve hot.
Makes 18.

TUNA AND CHEESE CANAPÉS

1 7¾-ounce can tuna fish, drained and flaked
1 cup (¼ pound) grated cheddar cheese

2 tablespoons dry sherry
¼ teaspoon freshly ground black pepper
4 slices buttered toast, quartered

Mix together the tuna, cheese, sherry and pepper. Spread on the toast squares. Bake in a 350° oven 5 minutes or until lightly browned and cheese slightly melted. Makes 16 canapés.

AVOCADO-TURKEY CANAPÉS

You will need equal quantities of trimmed thinly sliced white bread and pumpernickel. Spread the pumpernickel with mayonnaise mixed with dry mustard; then make sandwiches, using a thin slice of turkey or chicken, a thin slice of avocado and the white bread. Wrap in Saran or a damp towel and chill 2 hours, or until ready to serve. Cut in 4 strips or quarters.

ITALIAN PARMESAN CHEESE CANAPÉS

¾ cup grated Parmesan cheese
3 tablespoons heavy cream
¾ teaspoon Worcestershire sauce
6 slices crisp bacon, crumbled

8 slices buttered toast
16 pimiento-stuffed olives, cut in half

Mix together the cheese, cream, Worcestershire sauce and bacon. Trim the toast of the crusts and cut in 4 squares or triangles. Spread with the cheese mixture and put an olive half, cut side up, on each. Arrange in a baking pan and bake in a 400° oven 5 minutes, or until delicately browned. Serve hot.
Makes 32.

CHEESE DREAMS

1/3 cup milk
2 cups (½ pound) grated cheddar
  or American cheese
1 egg yolk, beaten

¼ teaspoon dry mustard
Dash cayenne pepper
Thin slices white bread
Melted butter

Bring the milk to a boil in the top of a double boiler. Mix in the cheese, then the egg yolk, mustard and cayenne pepper. Place over hot water and cook, stirring almost constantly, 15 minutes. Cool.

Cut 1-inch rounds or squares of white bread. Spread some cheese mixture on half the bread and cover with the remaining rounds or squares. Dip both sides in melted butter, arrange on a baking pan and bake in a 350° oven 10 minutes, or until browned and crisp. Serve hot. Any unused cheese mixture may be stored in a tightly closed container in the refrigerator.

Makes about 2½ cups, enough for about 32 canapés.

CHEESE-CAVIAR CANAPÉS

¼ pound Roquefort or blue cheese
3 tablespoons soft butter
2 tablespoons sour cream

6 slices white bread, trimmed
¼ pound caviar

Have the cheese at room temperature. Blend with the butter and sour cream until smooth. Spread on the bread and cover with the caviar. Cut each slice into 4 strips or squares. Arrange on a tray and garnish with lemon wedges.

Makes 24.

HAM AND CHEESE CANAPÉS

8 thin slices white bread
8 thin slices mozzarella cheese

4 slices cooked ham
4 tablespoons vegetable oil

Cut the crusts from the bread. On 4 slices of bread, place a slice of cheese, a slice of ham and then a slice of cheese over the ham. Cover with the remaining 4 slices of bread, making 4 sandwiches. Cut each sandwich into quarters.

Heat the oil in a skillet; brown the sandwiches in it on both sides. Drain. Serve hot.

Makes 16.

HOT DEVILED HAM-CHEESE CANAPÉS

2 4½-ounce cans deviled ham
1 tablespoon minced onions
8 slices toast, trimmed and cut in half

¾ cup grated cheddar cheese

Mix the deviled ham with the onions until smooth. Spread on the toast and sprinkle with the cheese. Place under a hot broiler until cheese melts.

Makes 16 canapés.

TARTAR STEAK CANAPÉS

½ pound lean fresh steak
½ teaspoon salt
¼ teaspoon freshly ground black pepper

⅛ teaspoon minced garlic
3 tablespoons minced onions
¼ teaspoon Worcestershire sauce

Lightly mix together all the ingredients. Shape into a mound. Serve with 2-inch rounds of pumpernickel or rye bread, capers, chopped onions and mustard.

Enough for 24 canapés.

SCHLEMMERSCHNITTE (Beef-Caviar Canapes, German Style)

10 slices buttered toast
1 pound freshly ground lean raw steak
¾ teaspoon salt

¼ teaspoon freshly ground black pepper
¼ pound caviar
¼ cup minced onions

Trim the crusts off the toast and cut in half diagonally. Season the ground steak with the salt and pepper and heap on the toast. Put a spoonful of caviar in the center of each and sprinkle with onions. If not to be served immediately, keep refrigerated.

Makes 20.

STUFFED ARTICHOKE CANAPÉS

½ pound crab meat
2/3 cup Russian dressing
½ cup teaspoon dry mustard

1 10-ounce can artichoke bottoms
Toast rounds (optional)
Chopped parsley

Pick over the crab meat, discarding any cartilage. Flake the crab meat. Mix the Russian dressing with the mustard and fold in the crab meat. Heap the mixture on the artichokes. Put each artichoke on a toast round, if desired, and secure with a toothpick. Arrange on a buttered baking pan and bake in a 475° oven, on the top level, 5 minutes. Sprinkle with parsley and serve hot.

Makes about 16.

TOASTED MUSHROOM CANAPÉS, POLISH STYLE

6 tablespoons butter
¾ pound mushrooms, coarsely
  chopped
¼ cup minced onions
1 tablespoons flour
½ teaspoon salt

¼ teaspoon freshly ground black
  pepper
½ cup sour cream
12 thin slices white bread,
  trimmed

Melt 2 tablespoons of the butter in a skillet; sauté the mushrooms and onions 5 minutes. Blend in the flour, salt and pepper; cook over low heat stirring steadily 1 minute. Gradually stir in the sour cream. Cook, stirring constantly until thickened. Taste for seasoning. Cool.

Make sandwiches of the bread and mushroom mixture. Cut into quarters and sauté in the remaining butter until browned on both sides.

Makes 24.

ONION-CHEESE CANAPÉS

Put a thin slice of onion on a toast round and sprinkle heavily with a mixture of grated Parmesan cheese, mustard and Worcestershire sauce. Or cover the onions with mayonnaise seasoned with curry powder. Sprinkle tops with grated Parmesan cheese. Arrange the canapés on a baking pan and broil until delicately browned.

CROSTINI DI POMIDORI (Italian Tomato Canapes)

4 tablespoons butter
¾ cup finely chopped onions
2 cups peeled chopped tomatoes
1 teaspoon salt
¼ teaspoon freshly ground black
   pepper

¼ cup grated Parmesan cheese
2 egg yolks, beaten
2 tablespoons minced parsley
5 slices toast, cut in half

Melt the butter in a skillet; sauté the onions 10 minutes. Add the tomatoes, salt and pepper. Cook over low heat 10 minutes or until no liquid remains. Cool. Mix in the cheese, egg yolks and parsley; taste for seasoning—the mixture should be spicy. Spread on the toast; arrange on a greased baking sheet. Bake in a pre-heated oven 10 minutes or until lightly browned. Serve immediately. Makes 10.

CANAPÉS AUX EPINARDS (Spinach Canapes, Provence Style)

3 pounds spinach or 3 packages
   frozen
2 tablespoons butter
1½ tablespoons flour
½ cup beef broth
¾ cup grated Gruyère or Swiss
   cheese

36 sautéed 2-inch bread rounds
2 tablespoons ground blanched
   almonds
3 tablespoons melted butter

Wash the fresh spinach in cold running water until water runs clear. Drain and remove the stems. Drop the spinach into a deep pan of boiling salted water and cook 5 minutes. Drain in a colander and rinse under cold water. Drain again. Or cook the frozen spinach as package directs, then rinse under cold water and drain again. Chop the spinach.

Melt the 2 tablespoons butter in a skillet. Add the spinach and cook over low heat, stirring steadily, until all the liquid is evaporated. Blend in the flour; add the broth gradually, stirring steadily to the boiling point. Cook over low heat 5 minutes, or until thickened. Mix in ½ cup of the cheese. Cool. Heap the spinach mixture on sautéed bread. Sprinkle with the remaining cheese, almonds and melted butter. Just before serving, place under a hot broiler until delicately browned.

Makes 36.

CANAPÉS AUX OEUFS (French Egg-Watercress Canapes)

6 hard-cooked eggs	2 teaspoons prepared mustard
1/3 cup melted butter	2 tablespoons grated onions
¾ teaspoon salt	14 thin slices white bread, trimmed
¼ teaspoon white pepper	¾ cup chopped watercress

Put the eggs through a Mouli grater or chop very fine. Mix in the melted butter, salt, pepper, mustard and onions. Spread on half the bread slices, sprinkle with the watercress, cover with the remaining slices and cut each sandwich into 4 strips.

Makes 28.

COLD

A COLD HORS D'OEUVRE, of course, is a great boon to the busy hostess. It may be prepared well in advance of the arrival of the guests, thus freeing the hostess for last-minute preparations and allowing her to be with her guests. If there is no domestic help, the cold hors d'oeuvre may be advisable for the novice hostess who feels that several hot dishes might be difficult to handle.

Some cold hors d'oeuvres should be served chilled, direct from the refrigerator; others are perfectly satisfactory at room temperature. In either case they may be prepared earlier in the day. Care should be taken, however, to see that they do not dry out or otherwise lose their taste or appearance by standing.

Of all cold appetizers, caviar is in a class by itself. Fresh caviar is extremely expensive, as everyone knows. There are many types of less expensive caviar, in glass containers, which perhaps do not duplicate the taste of the fresh, but which are quite satisfactory prepared in canapés, etc.

At a large cocktail party, assuming that a half-dozen different hors d'oeuvres are offered, two or three may be of the cold type. Thus the hostess will be free to concentrate on heating and serving the hot hors d'oeuvres; meanwhile the cold hors d'oeuvres may be placed around the room for self-service on the part of the guests.

Japan prepares an unusual cold appetizer, kamano miko, with onions and smoked salmon. The cold stuffed peppers of northern Italy, peperone alla Piemontese, are excellent for cocktail parties or to begin a dinner. A most unusual preparation is oignons à la Monégasque, onions in raisin sauce, a specialty of the tiny country of Monte Carlo.

CAVIAR

True caviar devotees prefer it without any garnish—just spread thickly on thin freshly made unbuttered toast. However, you can serve it surrounded with small bowls of sieved hard-cooked egg yolks, sieved hard-cooked egg whites, finely chopped onions, sour cream and lemon wedges. Serve the caviar on a bed of crushed ice, if possible.

SALMON-CAVIAR CORNUCOPIAS

12 slices smoked salmon	2 tablespoons minced onions
¾ cup sour cream	2 ounces (or more) caviar

Trim the salmon slices evenly and cut each in 2 triangles. Roll up into cornucopias. Mix together all the remaining ingredients. Stuff the cornucopias. Chill.
Makes 24.

FAGIOLI CON CAVIALE (White Beans and Caviar, Italian Style)

2 cups dried white beans	¼ teaspoon freshly ground black
2 teaspoons salt	pepper
¼ cup olive oil	½ cup black caviar

Wash the beans. Cover with water and bring to a boil; let soak 1 hour. Drain. Add fresh water to cover and bring to a boil; cover and cook over low heat 2 hours or until tender, adding the salt after 1 hour of cooking time. Drain. Mash the beans lightly and toss with the oil and pepper; cool. Mix in the caviar lightly. Serve with Italian bread.

Makes about 4 cups.

SPICED SPANISH OLIVES

1 can green Spanish olives, drained
¼ cup wine vinegar
¼ cup olive oil
2 tablespoons chopped chives

1 clove garlic, minced
1 teaspoon Spanish paprika
½ teaspoon peppercorns

Crush the olives until the pits show.

Combine the olives with the remaining ingredients and let stand at room temperature 3 hours, then chill. The flavor improves with standing. Makes about 1½ cups.

GREEK OLIVES

2 pounds small, pointed black
  Greek olives
Wine vinegar to cover

2 lemons, thinly sliced
2 cups coarsely chopped celery
Olive oil

Crush the olives until the pits show and cover them with the vinegar. Let stand two days.

Drain and pack into sterilized jars, arranging the olives alternately with layers of lemon slices and celery. Cover with olive oil and keep in a cool place (not the refrigerator) until ready to serve. Makes about 2 pints.

MIXED ITALIAN OLIVES

1 can green olives, drained
1 can black olives, drained
1 cup chopped celery
1 green pepper, chopped
1 sweet red pepper, chopped
1 clove garlic, minced

¼ cup olive oil
¼ cup wine vinegar
½ teaspoon freshly ground black
  pepper
1 teaspoon orégano

Crush the olives until the pits show and combine with the remaining ingredients. Let stand at room temperature two days, then put into sterilized jars. Seal and refrigerate.

Makes about 3 cups.

OLIVES WITH DILL, SCANDINAVIAN STYLE

3 cans large green olives, drained
3 cloves garlic, minced
½ teaspoon crushed dried red peppers
2 sprigs fresh dill, or 1 teaspoon dried dill weed

1 bay leaf
¼ cup olive oil
¼ cup wine vinegar

Crush the olives until the pits show.

Combine the olives with the remaining ingredients and let stand 24 hours in a cool place (not the refrigerator). Place in sterilized jars, seal and store in the refrigerator.

Makes about 3 cups.

CELERY PINWHEELS

1 bunch celery
¼ pound Roquefort or blue cheese
2 tablespoons butter

Cut off the leaves of the celery. Carefully separate the stalks, wash and dry. Cream together the cheese and butter. Stuff each stalk and, beginning with the heart, reshape the bunch. Wrap in wax paper and chill 2 hours. Cut in ¼-inch slices.

Makes about 24 slices.

Note: Other fillings such as pâté or fish may be used in place of the cheese.

STUFFED CELERY

2 bunches celery.

Separate the stalks of the celery. Use only the inner stalks. Remove the leaves, wash and dry. Stuff the stalks with any of the following mixtures, using a pastry tube, if desired, and chill until needed.

Red Caviar:

½ pound cream cheese
2 tablespoons grated onions
¼ teaspoon freshly ground black pepper

¼ cup chopped parsley
½ cup red caviar

Have the cream cheese at room temperature and beat until smooth. Blend in the onions, pepper, parsley and then the caviar.

Cheese Filling:

¼ round ricotta or cottage cheese
¼ pound Roquefort or blue cheese

2 tablespoons sour cream
1 teaspoon Worcestershire sauce

Beat all the ingredients together until smooth.

Anchovy-Egg:

4 hard-cooked eggs, sieved
8 anchovies, minced
3 tablespoons grated onions
3 tablespoons mayonnaise

1 teaspoon prepared mustard
¼ teaspoon freshly ground black pepper

Mix all the ingredients together until well blended.

Pate:

Use 8 ounces of any quality pâté, mashed smooth with a 3-ounce package of cream cheese and ¼ teaspoon freshly ground black pepper.

Tuna:

1 7-ounce can tuna fish, drained and flaked
2 tablespoons mayonnaise

¼ cup pickle relish
¼ teaspoon freshly ground black pepper

Mix all the ingredients together until well blended.

Deviled Ham:

¼ pound cream cheese
3 tablespoons prepared horseradish
2 3-ounce cans deviled ham

Mash the cream cheese smooth. Mix in the horseradish and ham.

CELERY CURLS

Separate a bunch of celery into individual stalks. Wash, and trim off the leaves. Cut a few long gashes in each stalk. Place in ice water until curled. Drain and dry.

PEPERONE ALLA PIEMONTESE (Stuffed Pepper Appetizer, Italian Style)

6 green and red peppers
1½ cups peeled cubed tomatoes
3 cloves garlic, sliced
½ cup minced anchovies

3 tablespoons dry bread crumbs
3 tablespoons olive oil
4 tablespoons butter

Red and green peppers may be used, or all green or red. Cut the peppers in quarters lengthwise; scoop out the seeds and fibers.

Mix together the tomatoes, garlic, anchovies, bread crumbs and oil. Stuff the pepper quarters. Arrange in an oiled baking pan; dot with the butter. Bake in a 375° oven 30 minutes or until crisply tender. Serve cold.

Makes 24.

OIGNONS À LA MONÉGASQUE (Onions in Raisin Sauce, Monaco Fashion)

1½ pounds small white onions
4 tablespoons olive oil
1½ cups water
½ cup wine vinegar
3 tablespoons tomato paste
1 bay leaf

¼ teaspoon marjoram
2 tablespoons sugar
½ cup seedless raisins
1½ teaspoons salt
½ teaspoon freshly ground black
    pepper

Select the onions all one size and as small as possible. Peel the onions. Heat the oil in a saucepan, add onions and toss until coated with the oil. Mix in the water, vinegar, tomato paste, bay leaf, marjoram, sugar, raisins, salt and pepper and bring to a boil. Cover and cook over low heat 30 minutes, shaking the pan frequently. Chill. Pierce with cocktail picks.
Makes about 40.

ONION SANDWICHES

8 brioches or 20 thin slices white bread	20 paper-thin slices sweet raw onion (red, if available)
½ cup mayonnaise	Salt
¼ cup sour cream	½ cup minced parsley

Slice the brioches into ¼-inch-thick rounds. You should have about 40 slices. Using a 1- or 1½-inch cooky cutter, cut out the centers. If bread is used, cut each slice into 2 circles.

Mix the mayonnaise with the sour cream. Spread a little on the brioche or bread. Have the onion slices the same size, and make sandwiches, sprinkling the onion with a little salt.

Roll the edges in the remaining mayonnaise mixture, and then in the parsley. Chill.
Makes about 20.

LEGUMI IN ACETO (Pickled Vegetable Antipasto, Italian Style)

1 8-ounce can button mushrooms, drained	1½ cups wine vinegar
	¼ cup sugar
1 green pepper, cut in ½-inch strips	1½ teaspoons salt
1 carrot, cut lengthwise into eighths	½ teaspoon freshly ground black pepper
2 cups cauliflower flowerets	
12 small white onions	1 teaspoon orégano
½ cup pimiento-stuffed olives	1 cup olive oil

Combine all the vegetables and the olives in a bowl. Heat the vinegar; stir in the sugar, salt, pepper and orégano until sugar dissolves. Cool slightly and mix in the oil. Pour over the vegetables and mix until vegetables are coated with the dressing. Cover and keep in the refrigerator at least 24 hours before serving. Drain and pierce with cocktail picks, or use as part of an antipasto plate.

Makes 4 cups.

ASPARAGUS ROLLS IN HAM

18 cooked or canned asparagus
¾ cup olive oil
¼ cup wine vinegar
½ teaspoon salt
¼ teaspoon freshly ground black pepper
¼ teaspoon basil
9 slices prosciutto or boiled ham

Marinate the asparagus in a mixture of the oil, vinegar, salt, pepper and basil 2 hours. Drain well. Cut each slice of ham in half crosswise. Wrap around an asparagus, fastening it with a toothpick.

Makes 18.

POMIDORI RIPIENI (Italian Stuffed Tomatoes)

36 cherry tomatoes (love apples)
1 can anchovy fillets
¼ cup chopped capers
1 clove garlic, minced
1 tablespoon olive oil
2 hard-cooked eggs, chopped
¼ teaspoon black pepper
1 teaspoon lemon juice

Cut off a small piece from the stem end. Scoop out the pulp carefully and chop it. Chop the undrained anchovies; mix with the chopped tomatoes, capers, garlic, olive oil, eggs, pepper and lemon juice. Stuff the tomatoes.

Makes 36.

RETTICH (Radishes with Spiced Butter, German Style)

16 radishes
¼ pound (1 stick) butter
2 tablespoons cream cheese
1 tablespoon grated onion
¼ teaspoon dry mustard
⅛ teaspoon Tabasco
Minced parsley

Buy firm, large radishes. Wash, dry, remove the leaves, but leave about ½ inch of stem and trim off the other end. Cut each radish in half, through the stem.

Cream together the butter and cheese, then blend in the

onion, mustard and Tabasco. Put ½ teaspoon of the mixture on each radish half or force through a pastry tube. Sprinkle lightly with parsley and chill.

Makes 32.

HOMMOS (Lebanese Chick-Pea Appetizer)

¼ cup lemon juice
½ cup sesame seed oil
1 clove garlic, minced
1 teaspoon salt

1 20-ounce can chick peas
½ teaspoon freshly ground black pepper
¼ cup chopped parsley

Beat the lemon juice into the oil very gradually, then beat in the garlic and ½ teaspoon of the salt.

Rinse the chick peas under cold running water. Drain. Purée in an electric blender or force through a sieve. Mix in the pepper, remaining salt and the sesame dressing. Spread on a flat dish, and sprinkle the parsley around the edge. Serve with crackers, toast or Arabian bread.

Makes about 2 cups.

FUNGHI ALL'OLIO (Italian Cocktail Mushrooms)

1½ pounds mushrooms
¾ cup olive oil
3 tablespoons lemon juice

1½ teaspoons salt
¼ teaspoon freshly ground black pepper

Buy very fresh, firm white mushrooms. Remove the stems and use for another purpose. Peel the caps and slice paper-thin. Mix together the oil, lemon juice, salt and pepper. Toss with the raw mushrooms. Chill 2 hours. Drain and surround with cocktail picks. Makes about 3 cups.

SHRIMP AND MUSHROOM APPETIZER

1 pound firm white mushrooms
½ cup olive oil
4 tablespoons lemon juice
½ teaspoon freshly ground black pepper

⅛ teaspoon minced garlic
1 pound shrimp, cooked, shelled and deveined
1¼ teaspoons salt
2 tablespoons minced parsley

Wash and dry the mushrooms. Remove the stems and use for another purpose. Quarter the caps; add the oil, lemon juice, pepper and garlic. Marinate in the refrigerator 2 hours, mixing frequently.

Thirty minutes before serving, mix in the shrimp and salt. Taste for seasoning and mix in the parsley. Spear a shrimp and mushroom on each cocktail pick. Makes about 24.

BOLOGNA-CHEESE WEDGES

¼ pound cream cheese
2 tablespoons light cream
2 teaspoons prepared horseradish

8 ⅛-inch-thick slices large
   bologna

Beat the cheese, cream and horseradish together until smooth. Make 2 stacks of 3 slices of bologna, spreading each slice with the cheese mixture. Cover each stack with the remaining bologna. Wrap in foil or wax paper and chill 4 hours. Cut each stack into 8 wedges and pierce each wedge with a cocktail pick.

Makes 16.

SALAMI CORNUCOPIAS

12 paper-thin slices salami
Watercress butter (see recipe)
Sprigs of watercress

Cut each slice of salami in half and roll up into a cornucopia. Fasten with a toothpick, if necessary. Fill with the watercress butter and chill 1 hour. Place a small sprig of watercress in each.

Makes 24.

DRIED-BEEF CORNUCOPIAS

¼ pound cream cheese
1 teaspoon prepared mustard
2 tablespoons grated onions

20 slices dried beef
Minced parsley

Beat the cheese, mustard and onions until smooth. Spread a teaspoon of the mixture on each slice of beef. Roll into a cornucopia and fasten with a cocktail pick. Sprinkle open end lightly with parsley.

Makes 20.

KAMANO MIKO (Pickled Smoked Salmon, Japanese Style)

12 slices smoked salmon	½ teaspoon dried ground chili
1 cup white vinegar	peppers
¼ cup water	½ pound small white onions
2 teaspoons sugar	2 tomatoes, cubed

Soak the salmon in cold water for 3 hours; drain. Cut in bite-sized pieces. Bring to a boil the vinegar, water, sugar and chili peppers. Slice the onions lengthwise. In a bowl or jar (not metal) arrange layers of the salmon, onions and tomatoes. Pour the vinegar mixture over it. Cover and let pickle in the refrigerator for 2 days before serving. Drain and heap in a bowl. Serve with toast.

Makes about 2 cups.

CALF'S FOOT JELLY APPETIZER

3 calf's feet or 1 steer's foot	1 tablespoon salt
2 cups sliced onions	¾ teaspoon black pepper
4 cloves garlic	4 hard-cooked eggs
4 quarts water	

Have the feet, bone and all, chopped up. Pour boiling water over them and scrape with a sharp knife to remove tough skin.

Combine the feet, bone and all, onions, garlic, water, salt and pepper in a kettle. Bring to a boil and cook over low heat 4 hours. Strain the soup. Cut the meat from the bones and divide among two or three shallow glass dishes. Pour the soup over the meat. Let it set for ½ hour, then slice the eggs and arrange in the dishes. Chill until firm. Cut into small squares and spear with picks.

Serves 8-10.

FIGS WITH PROSCIUTTO, ITALIAN FASHION

Buy ripe but unbruised figs. Wash, dry and cut off stems. Just before serving, wrap each fig in a slice of prosciutto ham. Secure with a cocktail pick. Sprinkle with freshly grated black pepper.

HAM BALLS

1 cup ground ham
1/4 cup mayonnaise
4 hard-cooked egg yolks, mashed
1/4 teaspoon freshly ground black pepper

1 tablespoon grated onions
2 tablespoons grated Parmesan cheese
1 cup ground nuts

Mix together all the ingredients but the nuts. Shape into walnut-sized balls and roll them in the nuts. Chill. Pierce each ball with a cocktail pick.

Makes about 24.

TARTAR STEAK BALLS

1 pound freshly ground lean steak
3 tablespoons minced onions
2 tablespoons minced parsley
1 teaspoon salt
1/4 teaspoon freshly ground black pepper

1/2 teaspoon prepared mustard
1 tablespoon anchovy paste
1 teaspoon A.1. Sauce
1 cup chopped walnuts or almonds

Mix together all the ingredients but the nuts. Shape teaspoons of the mixture into balls and roll them in the nuts. Chill 1 hour.

Makes about 32.

TONGUE PINWHEELS

1 3-ounce package cream cheese
2 teaspoons grated onions
2 teaspoons prepared mustard

2 tablespoons chopped green olives
12 thin slices cooked tongue

Mash the cheese smooth; blend in the onions, mustard and olives. Spread the mixture on the tongue slices and roll up like a jelly roll. Fasten with toothpicks and wrap in wax paper or foil. Chill. Cut in 1-inch slices.

Makes about 36.

STUFFED FRENCH BREAD SLICES

1 can anchovy fillets
½ pound cream cheese
1 tablespoon capers
2 tablespoons chili sauce
1 teaspoon grated onions

1 teaspoon Worcestershire sauce
Dash Tabasco
¼ pound (1 stick) soft butter
½ cup minced watercress
1 long loaf French bread

Mash the undrained anchovies to a paste. Beat the cheese until smooth. Mix in the anchovy paste, capers, chili sauce, onions, Worcestershire and Tabasco.

Cream the butter, then mix in the watercress.

Split the bread lengthwise and pull out the soft center. Fill the upper half with the watercress butter. Fill the lower half with the cheese mixture. Put the 2 halves together firmly. Wrap in foil or wax paper and chill 3 hours. To serve, cut into thin slices with a sharp knife.

Makes about 24 slices.

PROSCIUTTO RIPIENE (Stuffed Ham Rolls, Italian Style)

⅛ pound Gorgonzola or Roquefort
cheese
1 3-ounce package cream cheese

18 slices prosciutto ham
¼ cup minced parsley

Mash until smooth the Gorgonzola and cream cheese. Spread some on each piece of ham and roll up. Fasten with a cocktail pick and dip ends lightly in parsley. Makes 18.

HAM PÂTÉ ROLLS

1 3-ounce package cream cheese
2 ounces pâté de foie gras

8 paper-thin slices cooked ham
Minced truffles or parsley

Mash and beat the cheese smooth, then blend in the pâté. Spread the mixture on the ham and roll up each slice tight.

Chill 1 hour, then cut each roll in thirds. Dip the ends in truffles or parsley.
Makes 24.

HAM AND CHEESE ROLLS

2 tablespoons mayonnaise
1 cup grated American cheese
3 tablespoons chopped stuffed green olives

8 thin slices boiled ham

Mix together the mayonnaise, cheese and olives. Cut each slice of ham in 4, crosswise. Spread a heaping teaspoon of the cheese mixture on each piece. Roll up and fasten with cocktail picks.
Makes 32.

SMOKED SALMON ROLLS

8 slices smoked salmon
¼ pound cream cheese
2 tablespoons heavy cream

2 teaspoons curry powder
1 tablespoon grated onions

Buy large, thin slices of salmon. Beat the cheese, cream, curry powder and onions until smooth. Spread on one end of the salmon and roll up like a jelly roll. Wrap in aluminum foil or wax paper and chill. Cut ½-inch slices and serve on rounds of toast or crackers.
Makes about 36.

MINIATURE HEROS

8 Italian sausages, sliced
¾ cup sliced onions
3 green peppers, cut in half and diced

½ teaspoon salt
¼ teaspoon freshly ground black pepper
Italian bread

Cook the sausages in a skillet until they begin to brown. Pour off most of the fat. Add the onions, green peppers, salt and pepper. Cook over low heat 10 minutes, stirring frequently.

While the sausages are cooking, cut the bread in 2-inch slices, then cut each slice in half. Make miniature sandwiches with the sausage mixture.

Makes about 24.

OEUFS FARCIS (Stuffed Eggs, French Style)

10 hard-cooked eggs

While the eggs are cooking, turn them gently several times to keep the yolks in the center. Shell the eggs, and cut in half lengthwise, or cut in half crosswise, then cut a little of the white off each end so eggs can stand upright. Remove the yolks and mash very smooth; force through a sieve with selected ingredients or run in an electric blender with selected ingredients. Use a pastry bag to stuff the whites, or use a a spoon.

Anchovy-Stuffed Eggs:

4 anchovy fillets, finely chopped
2 tablespoons minced chives or scallions (green onions)
2 tablespoons mayonnaise

Mix all the ingredients with the 10 mashed hard-cooked egg yolks. Proceed as directed.

Caviar-Stuffed Eggs:

3 tablespoons sour cream
3 tablespoons black or red caviar
⅛ teaspoon white pepper

Mix the 10 mashed hard-cooked egg yolks with the sour cream. Carefully stir in the caviar and pepper. Stuff the eggs and garnish with a little caviar, if desired.

Chicken Liver-Stuffed Eggs:

4 chicken livers
2 tablespoons chopped onions
2 tablespoons butter
1 teaspoon salt
¼ teaspoon freshly ground black pepper

Sauté the chicken livers and onions in the butter for 5 minutes. Chop very fine and mix with the 10 mashed hard-cooked egg yolks and the salt and pepper or run in an electric blender. Taste for seasoning and proceed as directed.

Deviled Ham-Stuffed Eggs:

Mix ½ cup deviled ham with the 10 mashed hard-cooked egg yolks.

Pâté:

1 4-ounce can pâté
2 tablespoons cream cheese

Mash the pâté and cream cheese smooth. Proceed as directed.

Salmon-Stuffed Eggs:

4 tablespoons butter
½ cup canned salmon
2 teaspoons anchovy paste

1 teaspoon Worcestershire sauce
⅛ teaspoon freshly ground black pepper

Force all the ingredients and the 10 hard-cooked egg yolks through a sieve or run in an electric blender. Proceed as directed.

Olive-Caper Stuffed Eggs:

¼ cup minced Greek or Italian olives
8 anchovy fillets, minced
2 tablespoons capers

¼ cup tuna fish
3 tablespoons olive oil
1 teaspoon lemon juice

71

Chop together the olives, anchovies, capers and tuna fish. Add the 10 hard-cooked egg yolks and continue chopping. Gradually mix in the oil, then the lemon juice. Taste for seasoning and proceed as directed.

PICKLED EGGS

2 cups cider vinegar	1 teaspoon mixed pickling spice
1 cup water	2 tablespoons sugar
1 teaspoon salt	12 hard-cooked eggs
½ teaspoon celery seed	1 clove garlic, minced

Combine and bring to a boil the vinegar, water, salt, celery seed, pickling spice and sugar. Cook 5 minutes and cool.

Put the shelled eggs in a bowl or wide-mouthed jar. Strain the vinegar mixture over them and add the garlic. Cover tightly and let pickle in the refrigerator 3 days. Drain and dry. If desired, the eggs may be cut in half before serving. Makes 12.

OEUFS À LA HONGROISE (Eggs in Paprika Sauce, Hungarian Style)

2 tablespoons grated onions	½ cup mayonnaise
2 teaspoons paprika	¼ cup sour cream
½ teaspoon Worcestershire sauce	8 hard-cooked eggs
⅛ teaspoon freshly ground black pepper	

Blend together the onions, paprika, Worcestershire sauce, pepper, mayonnaise and sour cream. Cut the eggs in half and coat with the paprika sauce. Serve cold. Makes 16.

OEUFS CRESSONIÈRE (Eggs with Watercress, French Style)

6 hard-cooked eggs	2 tablespoons heavy cream
1 bunch watercress	½ cup mayonnaise

Quarter the eggs. Purée half the watercress in an electric blender with the cream, or chop to a paste, stirring in the cream gradually. Mix with the mayonnaise. Arrange eggs on a serving dish and cover each quarter with the green mayonnaise. Garnish with sprigs of the remaining watercress.

Makes 24.

CHILI NUTS

3 tablespoons butter
1 pound blanched nuts
2 teaspoons chili powder

Melt the butter in a skillet; add the nuts and cook over low heat, shaking the pan frequently, until browned. Turn out onto paper towels, and while hot, sprinkle with the chili powder, tossing to coat the nuts.

STUFFED NUTS

Mash Roquefort or blue cheese to a smooth paste with enough cream to make the mixture spreadable. Spread between 2 large walnut or pecan halves. The edges may be rolled in chopped parsley.

TOASTED NUTS

3 tablespoons butter
1 pound blanched nuts
Salt (optional)

Melt the butter in a baking pan. Add the nuts, tossing until nuts are coated with the butter. Bake in a 350° oven 30 minutes or until browned, shaking the pan frequently. Turn out onto paper towels and, while hot, sprinkle with salt if desired.

73

HOT

EVERY ASSORTMENT of hors d'oeuvres should include at least one hot variety. Unless you have special equipment, it is a good idea to heat only the number you think will be consumed immediately, so that they won't get cold. Usually an hors d'oeuvre that is supposed to be served hot, but which is offered when cold, is a disappointment. There is special electrical warming equipment available that will prevent this, of course, and if you entertain frequently, such appliances are worth-while investments. Chafing dishes, hot trays, etc., are both practical and decorative, so use them if at all possible.

Chinese Egg Rolls are not too difficult to prepare, and the homemade versions inevitably taste better than those encountered in restaurants. I was impressed in Naples, Italy, by the interesting hot appetizers made with cheese, such as calzone, prosciutto e mozzarella, and antipasto napoletana, all of which appear in this section. Indonesia's saté, spicy cubes of meat on skewers, is a superb hot hors d'oeuvre; you'll find interesting miniature skewers for sale in gourmet shops which make a delightful way to present this to your guests.

PÂTE FRIT (French Hors d'Oeuvre Fritters)

½ cup flour
¼ teaspoon salt
1 egg yolk
½ cup dry white wine or water

1 tablespoon melted butter
1 egg white
Vegetable oil for deep frying

Sift the flour and salt into a bowl. Beat the egg yolk, mix in the wine or water and add to the flour mixture, stirring only until smooth. Blend in the butter. Let batter stand 1 hour at room temperature. Beat the egg white until stiff and fold into the batter. Dip selected ingredients into the batter, coating them well, or fold in any of the following mixtures.

74

Heat the oil to 370°. Drop coated ingredients or teaspoons of the desired mixture into it and fry until browned on all sides. Don't crowd the pan. Drain on paper towels. Serve hot.

Makes about 36 fritters.

Beignets de Fromage (Cheese Fritters):
Fold ½ cup diced Swiss or Gruyère cheese into batter. Fry as directed.

Beignets de Crevettes (Shrimp Fritters):
Fold 1 cup diced cooked shrimp into batter. Fry as directed.

Beignets de Jambon (Ham Fritters):
Fold ¾ cup chopped ham, 1 tablespoon minced parsley and ¼ teaspoon freshly ground black pepper into batter. Fry as directed.

Beignets de Poisson (Fish Fritters):
Fold 1 cup chopped cooked fish or canned tuna fish, 1 tablespoon minced green onions and ¼ teaspoon freshly ground white pepper into batter. Fry as directed.

Beignets de Riz de Veau (Sweetbread Fritters):
Fold 1 cup finely diced cooked sweetbreads and 2 tablespoons chopped green olives into batter. Fry as directed.

RUSSIAN BUCKWHEAT BLINIS

2 cup buckwheat flour	1 egg, beaten
¾ teaspoon salt	2¼ cups milk
2 teaspoons baking powder	2 tablespoons melted butter
½ teaspoon baking soda	3 tablespoons butter

Sift together the buckwheat flour, salt, baking powder and baking soda. Add the egg and milk gradually, stirring until a smooth batter is formed, then mix in the melted butter.

Use a 'plattar' pan (a skillet with 2½-inch depressions) and melt a little butter in each. Pour about 1 tablespoon of batter into each and bake until browned on both sides. Keep pancakes warm while preparing the balance. (If you haven't a 'plattar' pan, use a skillet or a griddle and make 2½-inch cakes.)

Spread with caviar, sour cream and onions, then roll up. Or spread with any filling and roll up.

Makes about 32.

BLINIS AU CAVIAR (Blinis with Red Caviar, French Style)

2 cups sour cream
1 6-ounce jar red caviar, drained

1 tablespoon minced onion
Blini recipe

Mix the sour cream, caviar and onion.

Using 3 blinis for each serving, spread 2 with the caviar mixture and top with the third blini. Serve with melted browned butter, if desired.

Serves 4-6.

HORS D'OEUVRE CRÊPES

3 eggs
1½ cups sifted flour
½ teaspoon salt

1½ cups milk
Butter

Beat the eggs until light; sift in the flour and salt, then beat in the milk until very smooth.

A Swedish 'plattar' pan is excellent for making tiny crêpes. This is about an 11-inch pan, with 2½-inch circular depressions. Heat the pan and brush each section with butter. Pour in just enough batter to coat the bottom thinly. Bake until lightly browned on both sides. If you haven't a 'plattar' pan, heat a large skillet, brush with butter, and make 3-inch pancakes. Or you may make 6-inch crêpes, fill, roll and cut in half. Stack and keep hot while preparing the balance. Add butter as needed.

Makes about 36 3-inch crêpes.

HORS D'OEUVRE FILLINGS

Pâté:

1 4½-ounce can pâté de foie gras
3 tablespoons heavy cream

Mash the pâté smooth with the cream. Place a teaspoon of the mixture on each crêpe, roll up and fasten with a toothpick. Arrange on a serving plate and place in a 450° oven for 2 minutes.

Seafood Filling:

1 tablespoon butter
1 tablespoon flour
½ cup milk
¼ teaspoon salt
⅛ teaspoon Tabasco
½ cup chopped cooked shrimp
½ cup minced clams, well drained
¼ cup grated Parmesan cheese

Melt the butter in a saucepan; blend in the flour. Gradually add the milk, stirring steadily to the boiling point. Mix in the salt and Tabasco; cook over low heat 5 minutes. Cool. Mix in the shrimp and clams. Taste for seasoning. Place a teaspoon of the mixture on each crêpe. Roll up, fasten with toothpicks and arrange in a single layer in a buttered shallow baking dish. Sprinkle with the cheese. Place under a hot broiler until delicately browned.

Smoked Salmon Filling:

1 3-ounce package cream cheese
¼ cup sour cream
½ cup minced smoked salmon
⅛ teaspoon freshly ground black pepper
2 teaspoons curry powder

Beat the cream cheese and sour cream until smooth. Mix in the salmon, pepper and curry powder. Put a teaspoon of the

77

mixture on each crêpe. Roll up, fasten with a toothpick, arrange on a serving dish and place in 450° oven for 5 minutes.

Cheese Filling:

2 3-ounce packages cream cheese	1 egg white, beaten stiff
2 teaspoons prepared mustard	¼ cup grated Parmesan cheese
2 cups grated cheddar cheese	2 tablespoons butter

Beat the cream cheese and mustard until smooth and fluffy. Mix in the mustard and cheddar cheese. Fold in the egg white. Place a teaspoon of the mixture on each crêpe. Roll up, fasten with toothpicks and arrange in a buttered shallow baking dish. Sprinkle with the Parmesan cheese and dot with the butter. Bake in a 425° oven 10 minutes or until lightly browned and bubbly hot.

Provencal Filling:

2 anchovy fillets	1½ cups chopped ham
2 tablespoons minced onions	1 egg yolk, beaten
1 clove garlic, minced	¼ teaspoon freshly ground black
1 tablespoon minced parsley	pepper
1 tablespoon cognac	

Mash the anchovies to a paste; mix in the onions, garlic, parsley, cognac, ham, egg yolk and pepper. Let stand 15 minutes.

Place a teaspoon of the filling on each crêpe, roll up and fasten with toothpicks. Arrange in a shallow buttered baking dish. Place in a 375° oven for 10 minutes.

CRISP HORS D'OEUVRE CRÊPES

Prepare any hors d'oeuvre crêpe—fill, roll and fasten with toothpicks. Dip each crêpe in seasoned flour, then in beaten egg and finally roll in dry bread crumbs. Fry in deep 390° fat until browned. Drain.

CH'UN CHUAN (Chinese Egg Rolls)

Pancake Batter:

2 eggs
1 cup water
1 cup sifted flour

½ teaspoon salt
Vegetable oil for deep frying

Beat the eggs, then mix in the water. Add the flour and salt, beating until smooth.

Heat a 6-inch skillet and brush with oil. Pour in about 2 tablespoons batter, tilting the pan quickly to coat the bottom. Bake until browned on underside, then turn out, browned side up, onto a moist towel. Stack while preparing the balance of the pancakes. Reserve a little batter for sealing. Place a heaping tablespoon of any desired filling on each pancake, turn opposite sides in and roll up, sealing the edges with reserved batter. Heat the oil to 370° and fry the rolls until browned. Drain. Cut into thirds.

Shrimp Filling:

1 pound shrimp, cooked and cleaned
½ cup chopped water chestnuts
3 scallions, chopped
¼ cup chopped celery

2 eggs, beaten
1 tablespoon soy sauce
½ teaspoon salt

Chop the shrimp coarsely and mix with all the remaining ingredients. Fill the pancakes and fry as directed.

Pork Filling:

2 tablespoons vegetable oil
½ pound pork, diced fine
½ cup diced water chestnuts
¼ cup chopped scallions
¼ cup canned green peas

¼ cup chopped canned mushrooms
2 teaspoons soy sauce
¼ teaspoon pepper
½ teaspoon sugar
2 tablespoons minced parsley

Heat the oil in a skillet; sauté the pork until browned, about 10 minutes. Mix in the water chestnuts, scallions, green peas, mushrooms, soy sauce, pepper, sugar and parsley. Fill the pancakes and fry as directed.

SHRIMP-RICE CAKES

3 tablespoons butter
3 tablespoons flour
1 teaspoon salt
¼ teaspoon black pepper
1 teaspoon curry powder
¾ cup milk
1 cup cooked rice

½ cup grated cheddar cheese
3 tablespoons grated onions
1 pound shrimp, cooked, cleaned
   and diced
¾ cup dry bread crumbs
1 cup vegetable oil

Melt the butter in a saucepan; blend in the flour, salt, pepper and curry powder. Add the milk, stirring constantly to the boiling point. Cook over low heat 5 minutes. Remove from heat and mix in the rice, cheese, onions and shrimp. Taste for seasoning. Chill 1 hour. Shape into 36 patties. Roll in the bread crumbs. Heat the oil in a skillet until it bubbles. Fry the patties until browned on both sides. Drain and serve hot.

Makes about 36.

OYSTER-SAUSAGE BALLS

1 pint shucked oysters
¾ pound sausage meat
1½ teaspoons salt
½ teaspoon freshly ground black
   pepper

⅛ teaspoon cayenne pepper
2 tablespoons grated onions
1 egg, beaten
¾ cup dry bread crumbs
Vegetable oil for deep frying

Drain the oysters and chop fine. Mix with the sausage meat, salt, pepper, cayenne pepper, onions and egg until well blended. Shape into walnut-sized balls and roll in the bread crumbs.

Heat the oil to 360°. Fry the balls until browned on all sides. Don't crowd the pan. Drain, pierce with cocktail picks and serve hot, with hot chili sauce as a dip, if desired.

Makes about 48.

LOBSTER-ALMOND TOAST, CHINESE STYLE

2 tablespoons butter
2 tablespoons flour
1 cup light cream
¾ teaspoon salt
Dash cayenne pepper

1 egg yolk
1 tablespoon dry sherry
1 pound cooked lobster meat, diced
½ cup chopped blanched almonds
Buttered toast rounds

Melt the butter in a saucepan; blend in the flour. Gradually add the cream, stirring steadily to the boiling point. Stir in the salt and cayenne pepper; cook over low heat 5 minutes. Beat the egg yolk and sherry in a bowl; gradually add the hot mixture, stirring steadily to prevent curdling. Return to the saucepan and cook, stirring steadily, until thickened, but do not let boil. Mix in the lobster and almonds. Taste for seasoning. Heap on toast rounds.

Makes about 24 2-inch rounds.

Note: Shrimp or crab meat may be prepared in the same manner.

DROP CODFISH CAKES

1 pound salt codfish
3 cups hot mashed potatoes
1/8 teaspoon pepper

1 egg, beaten
Fat for deep frying

Wash codfish in cold water and let soak in water to cover 2 hours; drain, add fresh water, bring to a boil and cook 15 minutes. Drain, shred, and add to mashed potatoes with the pepper and egg; beat well. Drop by the teaspoon into deep 380° fat and fry until golden brown; drain on paper towels.

Makes about 36.

CRAB MEAT-BACON ROLLS

1 cup flaked crab meat
1 egg, slightly beaten
1/2 cup tomato juice
1 cup soft bread crumbs
1/4 teaspoon salt

1/8 teaspoon pepper
2 teaspoons chopped parsley
1 teaspoon chopped celery leaves
12 slices bacon

Combine crab meat, egg, tomato juice, bread crumbs, salt, pepper, parsley and celery leaves, mixing well. Shape into 12 finger-length rolls. Wrap each roll with a strip of bacon and fasten with toothpicks. Place on broiler rack and broil until bacon is crisp, turning frequently.

Makes 12 rolls.

CRAB MEAT-STUFFED MUSHROOMS

24 large mushrooms
3 tablespoons butter
¾ pound crab meat, flaked
¼ cup heavy cream

¼ teaspoon white pepper
1 teaspoon Worcestershire sauce
¼ cup grated Parmesan cheese

Wash, dry and remove the stems of the mushrooms. Melt the butter in a skillet; sauté the mushroom caps, hollow side up, 3 minutes. Transfer to a buttered shallow baking dish.

Mix together the crab meat, cream, pepper and Worcestershire sauce; stuff the mushrooms with the mixture and sprinkle with the cheese. Bake in a 375° oven 10 minutes or until browned. Pierce with cocktail picks and serve hot.

Makes 24.

SARDINE AND BACON ROLLS

2 cans skinless, boneless sardines
3 tablespoons mayonnaise
1 tablespoon grated onions

2 teaspoons prepared mustard
20 slices bacon (about)

Drain and mash the sardines. Blend in the mayonnaise, onions and mustard. Spread on the bacon slices, roll up, fasten with toothpicks and broil until the bacon is crisp. You may need more or less bacon, depending on how heavily you spread the sardine mixture. Drain and serve hot.

Makes about 20.

ANCHOVY PASTE ON TOAST, SICILIAN STYLE

3 cans anchovy fillets
2 tablespoons minced onions
2 cloves garlic, minced
3 tablespoons minced parsley

2 tablespoons olive oil
1 tablespoon lemon juice
Buttered toast rounds

Chop the undrained anchovies and mash to a paste. Mix in the onions, garlic, parsley, olive oil and lemon juice. Spread on the toast and place on a buttered baking pan. Bake in a 475° oven 5 minutes and serve immediately.

Makes about 18.

PETITS PÂTES PROVENCALE (Anchovy-Ham Appetizers)

1 can anchovy fillets
1 clove garlic, chopped
2 shallots, chopped
4 whole peppercorns
1 tablespoon finely chopped parsley
1 teaspoon chopped chives

1 tablespoon cognac
1 cup chopped ham
2 tablespoons softened butter
1 egg yolk
Pastry for a 2-crust pie

Drain the anchovies, reserving 1 tablespoon of the oil. Chop together the anchovies, garlic, shallots and peppercorns, then pound to a paste. Add reserved oil, parsley, chives and cognac. Mix well and let stand 10 minutes. Mix in the ham, butter and egg yolk.

Roll out the dough and cut into 3-inch rounds. Place 1 tablespoon of the filling in the center of each round, wet the edges of the dough, fold over into a half moon, and pinch together. Bake in a 350° oven 20 minutes, or until golden brown.

Makes about 20 turnovers.

SWISS HAM SANDWICHES

12 slices boiled ham
6 slices Swiss cheese (⅛ inch thick)
2 eggs, beaten

1 cup bread crumbs
4 tablespoons butter

Trim the ham of all fat. Cut the cheese a little smaller than the size of the ham slices. Place a slice of cheese between 2 pieces of the ham slices. Press down firmly. Cut in half. Dip in egg, then in bread crumbs, coating the sandwiches very well, especially on the edges. Melt the butter in a skillet. Sauté the sandwiches over medium heat until browned on both sides. Makes 12.

CALZONE (Italian Ham-Cheese Turnovers)

½ envelope yeast
1/3 cup lukewarm water
1 cup flour
¾ teaspoon salt

10 slices prosciutto or cooked ham
10 slices mozzarella cheese
¼ cup olive oil
1 teaspoon black pepper

Soften the yeast in the water. Sift the flour and salt into a bowl. Stir in the yeast mixture until a ball of dough is formed.

If too dry, add a little more water. Knead on a lightly floured surface until smooth and elastic. Place in a bowl, cover and let rise in a warm place 2 hours.

Roll out the dough paper-thin. Cut into 5-inch rounds. On one side of each round place a half slice each of ham and cheese, cut to fit. Sprinkle with the olive oil and pepper. Fold over the dough into a half moon. Seal the edges with a little water; be sure the ham and cheese are completely enclosed. Arrange on an oiled baking pan. Bake in a 400° oven 20 minutes or until browned. Serve hot. Makes about 20.

PROSCIUTTO E MOZZARELLA (Sauteed Prosciutto and Cheese, Italian Style)

6 slices mozzarella cheese
12 slices prosciutto or cooked ham
12 thin slices white bread, trimmed
½ teaspoon salt
½ cup dry bread crumbs

½ cup sifted flour
1 cup milk
2 eggs, beaten
1 cup olive oil

Place a slice of cheese between 2 slices of ham, and then place between 2 slices of bread. Cut each sandwich into 4 triangles.

Combine the salt, bread crumbs and flour on a piece of wax paper. Dip the sandwiches in the milk, then in the breadcrumb mixture, and finally the eggs. Heat half the oil in a skillet. Fry the sandwiches in it until browned, adding oil as necessary.

Makes 24.

ANTIPASTO NAPOLETANA (Neapolitan Appetizers)

8 thin slices bread
1 pound mozzarella or white American cheese
16 anchovy fillets

1 teaspoon orégano
¼ teaspoon freshly ground black pepper
¼ cup butter or olive oil

Toast bread on one side and cut each slice in half. Cut the cheese into ½-inch-thick slices, then into 4 by 2-inch pieces. Place 1 slice mozzarella, 1 anchovy fillet and a little orégano on toasted side of 4 half slices, sprinkle with a little pepper and cover with other slices, toasted side in. Melt butter or heat oil and fry the sandwiches in it until browned on both sides. Serve immediately.

Makes 8.

MINIATURE FLUFFY HAMBURGERS

1½ pounds ground beef
1½ teaspoons salt
½ teaspoon freshly ground black pepper
¼ cup minced onions

⅛ teaspoon thyme
3 tablespoons flour
1½ cups milk
½ cup heavy cream
4 tablespoons vegetable oil

Mix together the beef, salt, pepper, onions, thyme and flour. Use an electric mixer or wooden spoon, and very gradually beat in the milk and cream until absorbed. Cover and chill 2 hours. Form tablespoons of the mixture into hamburgers.

Heat 2 tablespoons oil in a skillet; fry the hamburgers about 2 minutes on each side. Add more oil as needed. Pierce with cocktail picks or toothpicks.

Makes about 40.

KÖTTBULLAR (Swedish Meatballs)

6 tablespoons butter
1 cup chopped onions
1 cup fresh bread crumbs
1 cup light cream
1 pound ground beef
½ pound ground pork
½ pound ground veal

2 teaspoons salt
½ teaspoon white pepper
¼ teaspoon nutmeg
2 eggs, beaten
2 tablespoons minced parsley
½ cup flour
2 cups heavy cream

Melt 2 tablespoons butters in a skillet; sauté the onions 10 minutes. Soak the bread crumbs in the light cream 10 minutes.

Mix together the beef, pork, veal, salt, pepper, nutmeg, eggs, parsley, bread crumbs and onions. Shape into 1-inch balls and roll in the flour. Reserve any leftover flour. Melt the remaining butter in a skillet; brown the balls in it on all sides, shaking the pan frequently to turn balls so they will keep their round shape. Transfer to a casserole. Blend 2 tablespoons flour into the butter remaining in the skillet. Gradually add the heavy cream, stirring steadily to the boiling point; cook over low heat 5 minutes. Pour the sauce over the meatballs and cook over low heat 15 minutes.

Makes about 48.

SATÉ (Spiced Meat on Skewers, Indonesian Style)

2 pound steak or pork	1½ teaspoons salt
3 tablespoons vegetable oil	½ teaspoon ground coriander
¾ cup ground Brazil nuts or almonds	½ teaspoon turmeric
	2 teaspoons grated lemon rind
½ cup minced onions	1 teaspoon sugar
1 clove garlic, minced	⅛ teaspoon Tabasco

Cut the meat in ¼-inch cubes and toss with the oil. Chop all the remaining ingredients to a paste and roll the cubes of meat in the mixture, coating them well. Divide and thread the meat on about 16 small skewers or toothpicks and let stand 15 minutes. Arrange on a broiling pan.

Broil steak 10 minutes, pork 15, turning the skewers frequently to brown all sides. Serve hot.

Makes about 16.

MEAT COCKTAIL FRITTERS

3 tablespoons butter	3 tablespoons grated onions
4 tablespoons flour	1½ cups ground cooked meat
1 cup milk	3 tablespoons minced parsley
1 teaspoon salt	1 cup dry bread crumbs
⅛ teaspoon Tabasco	2 eggs, beaten
½ teaspoon powdered ginger	2 cups vegetable oil
½ teaspoon dry mustard	

Melt the butter in a saucepan; blend in the flour. Add the milk, stirring steadily to the boiling point. Stir in the salt, Tabasco, ginger, mustard and onions; cook over low heat 5 minutes. Mix in the meat and parsley. Spread on a plate and chill.

Shape teaspoons of the mixture into balls. Roll in bread

crumbs, dip in egg, and roll again in bread crumbs. Heat the oil in a skillet until it bubbles. Fry the balls until browned. Drain, pierce with cocktail picks and serve with a spicy tomato or mustard sauce.

Makes about 30 balls.

CHIAO TZSU (Fried Chinese Dumplings)

Dough:

1½ cups flour
¾ cup boiling water

Mix the flour and boiling water until a dough is formed. If too dry, add a little more boiling water; if too sticky, a little more flour. Form into a ball, cover with a damp cloth and let stand 30 minutes.

Filling:

4 tablespoons vegetable oil	¼ teaspoon salt
¼ pound ground beef or pork	½ teaspoon ground ginger
¼ cup chopped green onions	2 tablespoons dry sherry
1 tablespoon soy sauce	1 cup water

Heat 2 tablespoons oil in a skillet; brown the meat in it. Remove from the heat and stir in the green onions, soy sauce, salt, ginger, and sherry. Cool.

Knead the dough on a floured surface until elastic. Form into a long roll about ¾ inch in diameter. Cut into 1-inch lengths, flatten with the hand and roll out each piece into 3-inch circles. Sprinkle with flour while rolling. The dough should be very thin at this point. Place 2 teaspoons of filling on each circle and fold over into a half moon, sealing the edges with a little water. Pinch the edges together.

Use two 8-inch skillets. Heat 1 tablespoon of oil in each. Arrange the dumplings in it in rows, being sure the edges touch. Fry until dumplings are browned on the bottom. Add ½ cup water to each skillet. Cover and cook over low heat until the water is absorbed. Turn out browned side up, and separate the dumplings. Serve hot, with mustard.

Makes about 20.

LIVERWURST BALLS IN BACON

1 pound liverwurst
1 tablespoon minced onions
1 tablespoon minced parsley
¼ teaspoon thyme
⅛ teaspoon grated lemon rind
18 slices bacon (about)

Mash the liverwurst very smooth and blend in the onions, parsley, thyme and lemon rind. Shape the mixture into marble-sized balls. Cut the bacon slices in half crosswise and wrap around each ball. Arrange on a rack in a pan and bake in a 425° oven 10 minutes, or until the bacon is browned and crisp. Pierce with cocktail picks.

Makes about 36.

MAR TAI YOK BENG (Chinese Batter-Fried Pork Balls)

1 pound finely ground pork
½ cup finely chopped green onions
½ cup chopped water chestnuts
2¼ teaspoons salt
¼ teaspoon white pepper
2 eggs
¼ cup flour
Vegetable oil for deep frying

Chop together the pork, green onions, water chestnuts, 1¼ teaspoons salt and the pepper until very fine. Shape into marble-sized balls. Chill 30 minutes.

Beat together the eggs and remaining salt. Stir in the flour until smooth. Dip the balls in the mixture. Heat the oil to 365°. Fry the balls in it 10 minutes, turning them to brown all sides. Drain well. Pierce with cocktail picks and serve.

Makes about 36.

PORK BALLS WITH GINGER

1 pound ground pork
1¼ teaspoons salt
1 cup chopped water chestnuts
¼ cup finely chopped crystallized ginger
1 egg, lightly beaten
½ cup cornstarch
Vegetable oil for deep frying

Mix together the pork, salt, water chestnuts, ginger and egg. Shape into walnut-sized balls and roll lightly in the cornstarch. Heat the oil to 375°. Fry the pork balls until browned and no pink remains. Drain and pierce with cocktail or tooth-picks.

Makes about 16 balls.

CHICKEN-LIVER HORS D'OEUVRE

6 chicken livers
2 tablespoons prepared mustard
2 tablespoons finely chopped olives

6 slices bacon, cut in half crosswise
¼ cup dry bread crumbs

Wash the chicken livers in cold water, remove any dis-colored spots and cut each in half; dip in a mixture of the mustard and olives. Wrap bacon around each piece, fasten with a toothpick and roll in the crumbs. Bake in a 425° oven 15 minutes.

Makes 12.

CHINESE CHICKEN IN PAPERS

3 whole chicken breasts
1/3 cup soy sauce
3 tablespoons vegetable oil
½ cup chopped green onions
¾ cup chopped mushrooms

¼ cup chopped water chestnuts
½ teaspoon powdered ginger
1 tablespoon dry sherry
Vegetable oil for deep frying

Remove the skin and bones of the chicken, and cut each breast in half. Cut each piece in half to make it thinner, then put between two sheets of wax paper and pound as thin as possible. You will now have twelve pieces. Pour the soy sauce over the chicken pieces in a bowl and let stand 15 minutes. Drain and reserve the soy sauce.

Heat the oil in a skillet; sauté the green onions, mushrooms and water chestnuts 3 minutes. Add the reserved soy sauce, the ginger and sherry. Cook 1 minute, then cool. Flatten the chicken pieces and divide the mushroom mixture among them, spreading it on only one side. Fold the chicken over and press the edges together.

Cut parchment paper or foil into 12 5-inch squares and place a piece of chicken on each. Fold over the paper, en-velope fashion, being sure the chicken is completely enclosed. Seal the edges. Chill 2 hours.

Heat the oil to 370°. Fry a few envelopes at a time for 6 minutes. Drain and serve in the papers. Makes 12.

PEPERONATA CON OLIVE E ACCIUGHE (Peppers and Olives, Naples Style)

6 large red or green peppers
½ teaspoon salt
½ cup olive oil
1½ cups pitted Italian or Greek olives

2 cloves garlic, minced
6 anchovy fillets, minced

Broil the peppers as close to the heat as possible until the skins turn black. Rub off the skins; cut the peppers into narrow strips, discarding the seeds and fibers. Sprinkle with the salt.

Heat the oil in a skillet; sauté the peppers 2 minutes. Mix in the olives, garlic and anchovies; cook 2 minutes. Serve hot with Italian bread. Makes about 3 cups.

CROQUETAS DE FRIJOL (Tiny Bean Fritters, Mexican Style)

1 10½-ounce can condensed black bean soup
½ cup sifted flour
1½ teaspoons baking powder

1 clove garlic, minced
¼ cup minced onions
Vegetable oil for deep frying

Blend the condensed soup with the flour, baking powder, garlic and onions. Heat the oil to 370°. Drop by the teaspoon into the fat and fry until browned. Drain. Serve hot.
Makes about 36.

FUNGHI ALLA PARMIGIANA (Cheese-Stuffed Mushrooms, Parma Style)

2 pounds mushrooms
½ cup grated Parmesan cheese
¾ cup dry bread crumbs
½ cup grated onions
2 cloves garlic, minced
3 tablespoons minced parsley

1 teaspoon salt
½ teaspoon freshly ground black pepper
½ teaspoon orégano
¾ cup olive oil

Buy large, even-sized mushrooms. Wash but do not peel them. Remove the stems and chop; mix with the cheese, bread crumbs, onions, garlic, parsley, salt, pepper and orégano. Stuff the mushroom cups.

Pour a little oil into a baking pan. Arrange the mushrooms in it. Pour the remaining oil over them, being sure to get a little on each mushroom. Bake in a 350° oven 25 minutes. Pierce with cocktail picks. Makes about 40.

ALLUMETTES AU FROMAGE (Fried Cheese Sticks, French Style)

2 cups sifted flour
½ teaspoon salt
2 tablespoons butter
1 egg yolk, beaten

1/3 cup ice water
1 pound Swiss cheese (one piece)
Vegetable oil for deep frying

Sift the flour and salt into a bowl. Cut in the butter with a pastry blender or 2 knives. Add the egg yolk, tossing lightly. Add just enough of the water to make a soft dough. Cut the cheese into strips ½ inch wide, 3 inches long and ½ inch thick.

Break off pieces of dough, and roll in long thin strips. Wrap around cheese sticks, covering the cheese completely. Seal ends well. Heat the oil to 380° and drop the sticks into it. Fry until golden brown. Drain well.

Makes about 24.

GOUGÈRE BOURGUIGNONNE (Cheese Puff Appetizers, Burgundy Style)

¾ cup water
4 tablespoons butter
½ teaspoon salt
1½ cups sifted flour

3 eggs
1 cup (¼ pound) cubed Gruyère or Swiss cheese

Bring the water, butter and salt to a boil. Add the flour all at once, stirring steadily with a wooden spoon over low heat until the mixture leaves the sides of the pan. Remove from the heat and let cool 5 minutes. Add 1 egg at a time, mixing after each addition until smooth. Mix in the cheese (the

91

cheese should be cubed, not grated). Drop by the tablespoon onto a baking sheet. Bake in a preheated 425° oven 15 minutes, or until browned. Don't open the oven door during the baking time, or the gougère will fall. Serve hot or cold.

Makes about 48.

FRIED MERINGUE PUFFS

2 egg whites	½ cup grated Parmesan cheese
¼ teaspoon salt	Vegetable oil for deep frying
Dash cayenne pepper	Paprika

Beat the egg whites, salt and cayenne pepper until stiff but not dry. Fold in the Parmesan cheese thoroughly.

Heat the oil to 375°. Drop the mixture into it by the teaspoon and fry until delicately browned on all sides. Drain on paper towels. Sprinkle with paprika and serve hot.

Makes about 24.

PUFFED CHEESE SQUARES

1 loaf unsliced white bread	¼ pound (1 stick) soft butter
2 cups (½ pound) grated cheddar cheese	½ teaspoon dry mustard
	½ teaspoon paprika

Trim the crusts off the bread and cut into 1-inch cubes. Place the cheese over hot water until softened; stir smooth. Remove from the heat and beat in the butter, mustard and paprika. Dip the bread cubes in the mixture, coating them heavily. Chill.

Arrange on a greased baking pan and bake in a 400° oven 5 minutes, or until lightly browned and puffed.

Makes about 48.

CHEESE POTATO CHIPS

Mix grated Parmesan cheese with a little cayenne pepper and sprinkle on potato chips. Bake in a 400° oven 5 minutes.

PÂTÉS

Pâtés are easy to make and offer an elegant touch to a cocktail party. Of course a really fine imported pâté de foie gras just turned out of a can may be served, but the homemade variety offers a wider choice. A pâté can be made in advance, as it will keep about one week in the refrigerator. Prepare the pâté in an attractive bowl or mold, and serve it in the mold or unmold it. Freezing seems to impair the flavor and texture slightly, but it may be done if necessary.

Thinly sliced French bread, or freshly made toast squares are perfect for serving with pâtés. Crackers have the wrong texture, and are usually of too definite a flavor. A pepper mill should be provided for those who like a sprinkling on top.

The custom of serving a delicious, flavorsome smooth paste made from livers undoubtedly originated with the French chefs of several centuries ago, but many other nations have their versions of this preparation. The Italian crostini de fegato and the Jewish gehokte lebor are both excellent.

CHICKEN-LIVER PÂTÉ

1 teaspoon rendered chicken fat or vegetable oil	¾ cup diced onions
2 pounds chicken livers	4 teaspoons salt
1½ cups heavy cream	1¼ teaspoons freshly ground black pepper
3 eggs	½ teaspoon ground ginger
¼ cup cognac	½ cup flour
¼ pound unrendered chicken fat	

Rub a 2-quart mold with the rendered chicken fat or oil. Wash the livers, removing any discolored spots.

Use an electric blender if you have one, and purée about a fourth of the livers at a time, together with some of the cream, 1 egg, some cognac, a little unrendered fat and onion, some of the salt, pepper, and ginger, and a little flour. Repeat until all the ingredients are used up. Or grind the livers with the onions and fat, then work in the other ingredients.

Turn into the mold, cover the top with a double thickness of aluminum foil, and place mold in a pan of water. Bake in a 325° oven 1½ hours. Cool, then chill.

Makes 1½ quarts.

MOUSSE DE FOIE DE VOLAILLE (French Chicken-Liver Mousse)

1½ pounds chicken livers
½ cup heavy cream
1½ teaspoons salt
½ teaspoon freshly ground black
  pepper

3 tablespoons grated onions
2 tablespoons cognac

Wash the livers thoroughly and remove any discolored spots. Cover with cold water, bring to a boil and cook over low heat 5 minutes or until no pink remains. Drain well. Purée in an electric blender with the cream, or force through a sieve. Stir in the salt, pepper, onions and cognac. Taste for seasoning. Pack into a crock or mold and chill for 4 hours. Serve with thinly sliced French bread or toast triangles. Makes about 2 cups.

ITALIAN HOT CHICKEN-LIVER APPETIZER

12 thin slices Italian or French bread
6 tablespoons butter
½ pound chicken livers
2 tablespoons minced parsley
½ teaspoon salt

¼ teaspoon freshly ground black
  pepper
2 anchovies, mashed
2 tablespoons dry white wine

Sauté the bread in 3 tablespoons butter until browned on both sides.

Wash the livers, cutting away any discolored spots. Chop fine. Melt the remaining butter in a skillet; sauté the livers and parsley 3 minutes, stirring almost constantly. Mix in the salt, pepper, anchovies and wine; cook 2 minutes, again stirring almost constantly. Spread on the sautéed bread. Serve hot. Makes 12.

GEHOKTE LEBOR (Chopped Chicken Livers, Jewish Style)

1½ pounds chicken livers	3 hard-cooked egg yolks
6 tablespoons rendered chicken fat	1¼ teaspoons salt
1 cup diced onions	½ teaspoon black pepper

Wash the livers; cut away connective veins and green spots. Dry the livers.

Heat 3 tablespoons of the fat in a skillet; brown the onions in it. Remove the onions. Cook the livers in the fat remaining in the skillet for 5 minutes, or until no red remains. Grind or chop together the onions, livers and egg yolks until smooth. Mix in the salt, pepper and remaining fat; taste for seasoning. Chill. Serve with crisp crackers or thinly sliced bread.

Makes about 4 cups.

CROSTINI DI FEGATO (Chicken-Liver Pate on Toast, Roman Fashion)

1 pound chicken livers	1 teaspoon salt
4 tablespoons butter	¼ teaspoon freshly ground black
¼ cup finely chopped onions	pepper
½ cup chicken broth	2 teaspoons drained chopped capers

Wash the livers, removing any discolored spots and connective tissues. Purée the raw livers in an electric blender or chop very fine.

Melt the butter in a skillet; sauté the onions until yellow and transparent. Add the broth; cook over medium heat 5 minutes. Stir in the livers, salt and pepper only until no pink remains; mix constantly. Remove from heat and add the capers. Chill. Spread on sautéed Italian or French bread.

Makes about 2 cups.

PÂTÉ MAISON (Pate, French Peasant Style)

2 pounds calf's or beef liver, sliced	¾ teaspoon freshly ground black
½ pound bacon, diced	pepper
1 clove garlic, minced	1/3 cup cognac
½ cup chopped onions	4 thin slices salt pork
2 teaspoons salt	

Cook the liver, bacon, garlic and onions in a skillet 5 minutes. Purée in an electric blender or force mixture through a food mill. Blend in the salt, pepper and cognac. Pack mixture into a 9-inch loaf pan. Arrange the salt pork slices on top. Cover pan with aluminum foil. Place in a pan of water and bake in a 375° oven for 1¼ hours. Chill in the pan, turn out and slice ½ inch thick.

Makes 18 slices.

QUICK PÂTÉ

1/3 cup rendered chicken fat or butter
½ cup minced onions
1 pound liverwurst (goose, if possible)

3 tablespoons cognac
3 tablespoons heavy cream
¼ teaspoon freshly ground black pepper

Melt the fat in a skillet; sauté the onions 10 minutes, stirring frequently. Remove the casing of the liverwurst, and beat smooth with the onions, gradually adding the cognac and cream. Mix in the pepper. Taste for seasoning. Use in place of other pâtés or chopped-liver spread.

Makes about 1½ cups.

PÂTÉ À LA CAMPAGNE (Chicken Liver and Sausage Pate, French Country Style)

1½ pounds chicken livers
¾ pound sausage meat
1 cup sliced onions
¾ cup parsley
2 teaspoons salt
¾ teaspoon freshly ground black pepper

⅛ teaspoon thyme
½ cup rendered chicken fat, melted butter or bacon fat
2 eggs

Put the uncooked livers, sausage meat, onions and parsley through the fine blade of a food chopper. Mix in the salt, pepper, thyme, melted fat and eggs until well blended. Pack into a greased 10-inch loaf pan. Cover with aluminum foil. Set in a shallow pan of hot water and bake in a 275° oven 2 hours. Cool and unmold. Serve with French bread.

Serves 10-12.

PÂTÉ DE PORC (French Pork Pate)

1½ pounds fat boneless pork
1 pound calf's liver
½ cup finely chopped onions
1 clove garlic, minced
2½ teaspoons salt
¾ teaspoon freshly ground black
pepper

½ teaspoon marjoram
2 eggs
3 tablespoons cognac
3 tablespoons flour
8 thin slices salt pork

Put the pork and liver through the fine blade of a food chopper twice. Mix in the onions, garlic, salt, pepper and marjoram. Beat in the eggs, cognac and flour.

Line a 9-inch loaf pan with 5 slices of salt pork. Pour the pork mixture into it and arrange the remaining salt pork on top. Cover the top of the pan with foil, sealing the edges well. Place in a pan containing 4 inches of hot water. Bake in a 350° oven 2¼ hours. Let cool, covered, for 15 minutes. Place a weight on top and let cool completely before turning out.

Serves 10-12.

TERRINE DE PORC ET VEAU (Pork and Veal Pate)

½ pound round of veal
2 truffles
3 tablespoons cognac
1¾ teaspoons salt
½ teaspoon freshly ground black
pepper
Dash ground cloves
½ pound sliced salt pork
2 tablespoons butter

½ cup minced onions
½ cup port wine
¾ pound ground lean veal
¾ pound ground lean pork
½ pound fresh pork fat
2 eggs, beaten
½ teaspoon thyme
Dash ground allspice
1 bay leaf

Cut the round of veal into ¼-inch-thick strips. Cut the truffles into julienne strips. Marinate the veal and truffle strips in a mixture of the truffle liquid, cognac, ¼ teaspoon of the salt, ⅛ teaspoon pepper and the cloves. Cover the salt pork with boiling water, let stand 10 minutes, drain and dry.

Melt the butter in a skillet; sauté the onions 10 minutes, stirring frequently and without browning. Add the port and cook over high heat until reduced to half.

Put the ground veal, pork and pork fat through the food

97

chopper, using the fine blade. Combine with the onion mixture, eggs, thyme, allspice and the remaining salt and pepper. Beat with a wooden spoon until the mixture is very smooth. Drain the marinade from the veal and truffles and beat it into the meat and onion mixture. Cook a teaspoon of the mixture 5 minutes, then taste it for seasoning. Season the mixture if necessary.

Use a 2-quart oval casserole or loaf pan. Line the bottom and sides with the blanched salt pork, reserving some for the top. With wet hands, press ⅓ the ground mixture on the bottom of the dish. Arrange half the marinated veal strips over it with half the truffles in a strip in the middle. Repeat the layers, ending with the ground mixture. Put the bay leaf on top and cover with the reserved salt pork. Put a piece of foil on top, then cover with the lid. Place the mold in a pan of boiling water reaching halfway up the mold. Bake in a 350° oven on the lower level 1½ hours, or until the pâté has shrunk slightly away from the sides of the mold.

Remove the mold from the oven and place in a shallow pan. On the foil-topped pâté, put a plate or casserole that will just fit. Place a weight on top that is heavy enough to press down the pâté. Cool 3 hours at room temperature, then put in the refrigerator overnight, still weighted down.

The pâté may be served from the mold or unmolded onto a serving dish. In either case, slice and serve with French bread.

Makes 2 quarts.

LIVERWURST PÂTÉ

½ pound liverwurst	3 tablespoons cognac
1 3-ounce package cream cheese	⅛ teaspoon nutmeg

Remove the casing of the liverwurst and mash smooth with the cream cheese, cognac and nutmeg. Serve with thinly sliced French bread.

Makes about 1½ cups.

PASTRY

HORS D'OEUVRES prepared in pastry are marvelous, in that they are self-contained and require no other base or embellishment. They can all be frozen, permitting preparation in advance at your leisure, and then baked just before serving time. The contrast of flaky pastry and a tasty filling supplies an interesting difference in texture.

When filling baked pastry shells, you will find the use of a pastry bag a great aid; it provides a more professional, finished presentation. If the pastries are to be served hot, keep them on a hot tray, or else pass small quantities at a time and replenish them as needed.

Not all countries make use of pastry appetizers, but France and Italy are particularly renowned for their flaky, mouth-melting bits of pastry wrapped around well-flavored ingredients. In most of South America they make miniature pies or turnovers called empanaditas (Spanish) or empadinhas (Portuguese), customarily filled with meat or shellfish. The Russians are known for piroshki, tiny hot pastries filled with meat, mushrooms or the like. In the Middle East, sambousiks are similar to the South American empanaditas, but the fillings are usually flavored with curry.

RICH HORS D'OEUVRE PASTRY

2½ cups flour
1½ teaspoons salt
½ pound (2 sticks) softened butter

2 eggs
4 hard-cooked egg yolks, mashed

Sift the flour and salt into a bowl. Make a well in the center, and into it put the butter, eggs, and hard-cooked egg yolks. Work the ingredients in the well to a paste with the fingers, then gradually work in the flour until a smooth dough is formed. Form into a ball, wrap and chill 3 hours.

When ready to use, divide dough in half and roll out each half between two sheets of wax paper to desired thickness. Use as directed in recipes.

CREAM CHEESE PASTRY

1 cup sifted flour
¼ teaspoon salt

¼ pound (1 stick) butter
¼ pound cream cheese

Sift together the flour and salt. Cream the butter and cream cheese until soft and well blended. Work in the flour until smooth. Form into a ball, wrap in foil or wax paper and chill 2 or more hours. Roll out on a lightly floured surface to desired thickness and proceed as directed. Bake in a preheated 425° oven 12 minutes or until delicately browned.

Seed-topped Shapes:

Roll out the pastry ⅛ inch thick. Cut into 1-inch circles, triangles or squares. Brush the tops with beaten egg or heavy cream and dip in poppy, sesame or caraway seeds.

Pinwheels:

Roll out the pastry ⅛ inch thick. Cut into strips 6 inches wide. Spread with a selected filling and roll up like a jelly roll. Cut into ¼-inch slices.

Filled Fingers:

Roll out the pastry ⅛ inch thick. Spread half with a selected filling and fold the pastry over, pressing down gently. Cut into small finger lengths.

Palm Leaves:

Roll out the pastry ⅛ inch thick. Cut into strips 5 inches wide. Fold long edges to the center and press down gently. Fold again to the center, then cut into ¼-inch slices.

SOUR CREAM PASTRY

2 cups sifted flour
½ teaspoon salt

½ pound (2 sticks) sweet butter
6 tablespoons sour cream

Sift the flour and salt into a bowl; work in the butter with the hand, then the sour cream until well blended. Form into a ball and chill overnight or at least 2 hours. Use as directed in recipes.

PÂTÉ FEUILLETÉE (French Puff Paste)

1 pound (4 sticks) sweet butter	1 teaspoon salt
4 cups flour	1 cup ice water

Reserve 2 tablespoons of the butter and shape the rest into a flat, square cake about ½ inch thick. Dip lightly in flour. Chill. Sift the flour and salt into a bowl and work in the 2 tablespoons butter with the fingers. Gradually add just enough of the water, mixing with the hand, until a pliable ball is formed. (It may not be necessary to add all the water.)

On a lightly floured surface, roll out the dough into a ½-inch-thick rectangle about 10 by 16 inches. Put the chilled butter in the center. Fold over one side of the dough and then the other, completely covering the butter. Press the edges together. Wrap in a cloth and chill 20 minutes.

Put the chilled dough on the floured surface with one of the pressed ends toward you. Carefully roll out into a rectangle again, being sure the butter doesn't break through. Fold over into thirds, turn one open end toward you and roll out again (this is called a turn). Make 2 more turns. Fold into thirds again and chill 20 minutes. Repeat the rolling and chilling process twice more. Use pastry as directed in recipes.

PETITES BOUCHÉES (Miniature Patty Shells, French Fashion)

Puff Paste recipe

Roll out the puff paste ¼ inch thick and cut into 1½-inch rounds with a fluted cooky cutter. Cut out the centers of half the rounds to make rings. Reserve the cutouts. Brush the edges of the 1½-inch rounds with water and gently press a ring on top.

Line a baking sheet with lining paper or grease the pan and dust lightly with flour. Arrange the rounds on it. Gently place the cutouts in the centers. Chill 15 minutes. Bake in a 450° oven 10 minutes. Reduce the heat to 350° and bake 5 minutes longer, or until delicately browned. Carefully remove the cutouts. Fill as desired, replace tops and serve reheated or at room temperature.

Makes about 48.

ALLUMETTES (Miniature Napoleons)

Puff Paste recipe

Roll out puff paste ⅜ inch thick and cut into long strips 2 inches wide. Brush with beaten egg. Spread or put one of the fillings suggested at ½-inch intervals and cover with another strip of puff paste. Press down gently with the finger between each mound of filling, brush with egg, and with a pastry wheel or sharp knife cut at the depressions, so that each piece contains filling. Arrange on baking sheets and chill 15 minutes. Bake in a 425° oven 12 minutes or until puffed and browned.

Fillings:
Pâté de Foie Gras
Anchovies
Shrimp paste
Mushroom Filling
Lobster Spread

BARQUETTES (Small Pastry Shells)

Rich Hors d'Oeuvre Pastry recipe

Use small barquette tins (oval-shaped) or 2-inch round tart pans. Roll out the pastry ¼ inch thick between two sheets of wax paper. Cut the pastry a little larger than the pans and fit into the pans, allowing a little to hang over. Dip a small piece of dough in flour, and use it to press the dough gently against the bottom of the pans. Press the edges down lightly, then carefully trim off the overhanging dough. Chill the lined pans in a freezer or freezing compartment of the refrigerator 30 minutes. Prick the bottoms. Bake in a preheated 350° oven on the center level 10 minutes, or until delicately browned. Cool, then loosen the shells from the pans and turn out. Fill as desired.

Makes about 20.

Fillings:

Caviar garnished with chopped hard-cooked egg yolks and sour cream.

Seafood Spread
Smoked Salmon Spread
Tuna Spread
Green Caviar
Fresh Salmon Spread
Pâté or Chopped Liver

Any other mixture in the spread section may also be used.

SPINACH FILLING

3 pounds spinach
¼ pound (1 stick) butter
3 cups sliced green onions
¾ cup chopped parsley
½ cup chopped dill

1¼ teaspoons salt
¼ teaspoon freshly ground black pepper
½ cup sliced blanched almonds or pine nuts

Cut the stems off the spinach; wash thoroughly and dry. Melt the butter in a skillet; mix in the spinach and cook over high heat 2 minutes, stirring a few times. Add the green onions, parsley, dill, salt and pepper. Cook over high heat, stirring frequently until the liquid has evaporated. Chop the mixture, then cool. Taste for seasoning and mix in the nuts. Use for pastries, sponge roll, etc.

Makes about 2 cups.

ONION FILLING

¼ pound (1 stick) butter
6 cups diced onions
1 cup chopped green onions
1½ teaspoons salt
¼ teaspoon freshly ground black pepper
½ teaspoon sugar

Melt the butter in a skillet; add all the remaining ingredients, stirring well. Cover and cook over low heat 10 minutes. Remove cover and cook 10 minutes longer, stirring frequently. Taste for seasoning and cool. Use for pastries and strudel.

Makes about 3 cups.

CABBAGE FILLING

6 cups finely shredded cabbage
2 teaspoons salt
¼ pound (1 stick) butter
¾ cup minced onions
1 teaspoon sugar
¼ teaspoon freshly ground black
pepper

Sprinkle the cabbage with the salt; mix well and let stand 30 minutes. Drain. Melt the butter in a deep skillet; add the cabbage, onions, sugar and pepper and mix well. Cover and cook over low heat 10 minutes. Remove the cover and cook 30 minutes, or until cabbage is lightly browned. Stir frequently and add a little more butter if necessary. Taste for seasoning and cool. Use for pastries, kulebyaka and strudels.

Makes about 2½ cups.

MEAT OR POULTRY FILLING

5 tablespoons butter
¾ cup chopped onions
2 cups chopped cooked meat or
poultry
½ cup minced parsley

2 eggs, beaten
¾ teaspoon salt
¼ teaspoon freshly ground black
pepper

Melt the butter in a skillet; sauté the onions 10 minutes, stirring frequently. Add the meat or poultry; cook 2 minutes. Mix in the parsley, eggs, salt and pepper. Taste for seasoning. Use for pastries, barquettes, sponge rolls, kulebyaka, etc.

Makes about 2¼ cups.

Variation:

Curried Meat Filling

Add ¼ cup chopped chutney and 1 tablespoon curry powder to the meat mixture.

HAM FILLING

3 tablespoons butter	¾ cup sour cream
1 cup minced onions	2 egg yolks, beaten
2 cups chopped cooked ham	3 tablespoons chopped parsley
¼ teaspoon freshly ground black pepper	

Melt the butter in a skillet; sauté the onions 10 minutes, stirring frequently. Add the ham; cook 3 minutes, stirring occasionally. Remove from the heat and mix in the pepper, sour cream, egg yolks and parsley. Taste for seasoning, and cool. Use for pastries, barquettes, kulebyaka and strudel.

Makes about 2¼ cups.

SPONGE ROLL SLICES

4 egg whites	4 egg yolks
½ teaspoon salt	¼ cup sifted cornstarch
⅛ teaspoon cream of tartar	½ cup sifted flour
1 teaspoon curry or chili powder (optional)	

Grease an 11 by 16-inch jelly-roll pan, line with wax paper and grease the paper.

Beat the egg whites, salt and cream of tartar (and spice, if desired) until very stiff. Beat the egg yolks lightly. Add about ½ cup of the beaten whites and fold together thoroughly; pour this mixture over the remaining egg whites, then sift the cornstarch and flour over the top. Fold together gently only until no white patches remain. Spread in the lined pan evenly. Bake in a 400° oven 10 minutes or until delicately browned and a cake tester comes out almost dry. Do not overbake.

Cool pan on a cake rack 10 minutes, run a spatula under the paper and carefully turn out onto the rack until completely cool. Cut the sponge in half lengthwise. Spread with a desired filling, and roll up like a jelly roll, making a 16-inch-long roll. Wrap in foil or wax paper and chill 2 hours, then cut in ¼- to ½-inch slices and, if to be served hot, arrange on a greased baking sheet, cut side down. Bake in a 350° oven 8 minutes. Serve hot.

Makes about 9 dozen slices.

Caviar:

Spread each roll with ½ cup sour cream, ½ to ¾ cup black or red caviar, and 2 sieved hard-cooked egg yolks. Roll up. Chill as directed, slice and serve.

Pâté:

Spread each roll with 1 cup mashed pâté or chicken-liver spread (see recipe). Roll up, chill as directed, slice and heat as directed.

Ham:

Spread each roll with 1 cup ham spread (see recipe). Roll up, chill as directed, slice and heat as directed.

Chicken:

Spread each roll with 1 cup chicken spread (see receipe). Roll up, chill as directed, slice and heat as directed.

Cheese:

Mix together 2 cups grated cheddar cheese, ¼ cup chopped olives and ¼ cup heavy cream. Divide mixture between the two rolls. Roll up, chill as directed, slice and heat as directed.

Note: All the filled rolls but the caviar may be kept frozen for three weeks.

COCKTAIL PIZZA

1 package yeast
1 cup lukewarm water
1½ tablespoons vegetable oil
¾ teaspoon salt
3 cups sifted flour (about)
2 pounds tomatoes
¼ pound Italian sausage

2 tablespoons olive oil
1 teaspoon orégano
1 teaspoon basil
½ teaspoon freshly ground black
   pepper
¾ pound mozzarella cheese, sliced
1 can anchovy fillets, drained

Soften the yeast in the lukewarm water. Mix in the vegetable oil, ¼ teaspoon of the salt and 2¾ cups of the flour. The dough should be soft but not sticky. Add a little more flour if necessary. Turn the dough onto a floured surface and knead until very smooth and elastic. This will take about 10 minutes. Place in a greased bowl, brush the top with oil, cover with a towel and let rise in a warm place until double in bulk, about 1½ hours.

While the dough is rising, prepare tomatoes. Peel tomatoes and cut each into 6 wedges. Combine with the remaining salt, cover and cook over low heat 10 minutes or until very soft. Drain and reserve solid part.

Cook the sausage in a little water 5 minutes. Drain and continue cooking until lightly browned. Slice the sausage and reserve.

Grease a 15 by 10 by 1-inch jelly-roll pan.

Turn the dough out of the bowl onto a floured surface and shape into a ball. Roll the dough into a long strip that is about the length of the pan.

Place the dough in the pan and press and stretch with the fingers until the dough covers the sides of the pan. Spread the tomatoes over the dough and sprinkle with the olive oil, orégano, basil and pepper.

Arrange the sausage over ⅓ of the dough and cheese over the other ⅔. Arrange the anchovies over half of the cheese-covered dough, leaving the other half with cheese only.

Bake in a 500° oven on the lower shelf of the oven 15 minutes or until browned. Cut into 2-inch squares or bars and serve hot.

Makes about 36.

107

Anchovy:

1 2-ounce can anchovy fillets
2 tablespoons olive oil
1½ cups thinly sliced onions
1 20-ounce can tomatoes, drained and chopped

1 teaspoon salt
½ teaspoon freshly ground black pepper
½ teaspoon orégano
¼ cup grated Parmesan cheese

Pour the oil from the anchovy can into the olive oil. Cut each fillet in 4 pieces. Have the dough in the pan, brush the top with the oil. Make about 36 depressions in the dough and into each put a piece of anchovy. Arrange the onions over the dough, then spread the tomatoes over the onions. Sprinkle with the salt, pepper, orégano and cheese. Let rise and bake as directed.

Onion-Olive:

¼ cup olive oil
2 cups thinly sliced onions
¾ teaspoon salt
¼ teaspoon freshly ground black pepper

1 cup sliced black olives (Italian or Greek)
¼ teaspoon orégano

Heat the oil in a skillet; sauté the onions 5 minutes, stirring frequently. Mix in the salt and pepper. Cool 10 minutes, then spread over the dough. Sprinkle with the olives and orégano.

Bake as directed.

COCKTAIL KULEBYAKA (Russian Filled Pastries)

1 package yeast
¼ cup warm water
2¼ cups sifted flour
½ teaspoon salt
1 teaspoon sugar
3 eggs
⅜ pound (1½ sticks) soft butter
¼ cup melted butter
¾ cup cooked rice

4 hard-cooked egg yolks, sieved
1 cup sour cream
12 slices smoked salmon, cut in thirds
1½ cups chopped cooked shrimp
4 tablespoons chopped dill
Freshly ground black pepper
1 egg yolk, beaten

Soften the yeast in the water. Sift 1¾ cups of the flour, the salt and sugar onto a board. Make a well in the center, and into it put the eggs. Gradually work the flour into the eggs, until a soft dough is formed. Knead the dough 5 minutes, then pick up the dough and slap it down for 5 minutes. Work the 1½ sticks butter into the dough, then the yeast and remaining flour. Knead again until smooth, then put in a greased bowl. Cover with a towel and let rise in a warm place 1½ hours. Punch down the dough, knead lightly and return to the bowl. Cover the bowl and place in the freezer or freezing compartment for 1 hour.

Roll out the dough on a lightly floured surface and cut into 2-inch squares or rounds (you should have about 36). Brush each piece with melted butter. On one half of each, sprinkle some rice, hard-cooked egg yolks, and ½ teaspoon of sour cream, then put on each a piece of salmon, some shrimp, sour cream again, dill and pepper. Fold the dough over and seal the edges.

Arrange the pastries on a buttered baking pan. Cover and let rise in a warm place 20 minutes. Brush tops with beaten egg yolk and bake in a 400° oven 20 minutes, or until golden brown. Serve warm.

Makes about 36.

Variations:

Sausage

Brush squares or rounds with melted butter and put a 2-inch piece of cooked spicy sausage in the center. Bring the edges together and press to seal. Between the hands, form into an oval shape. Let rise and bake as directed.

Cabbage

Brush squares or rounds of dough with melted butter and put a spoon of cabbage filling (see recipe) on each. Fold over the dough, seal edges, let rise and bake as directed.

Liver

Brush squares or rounds of dough with melted butter and put a spoon of chopped liver (see recipe) on each. Fold over the dough, seal edges, let rise and bake as directed.

CROUSTADES (Toasted Bread Shells)

Use a loaf of unsliced white bread and trim off the crusts. Slice the bread 1 inch thick and then cut into 1½-inch rounds or squares. With a very sharp, pointed knife, cut out some of the center, leaving a bottom about ¼ inch thick. Brush the sides and tops heavily with melted butter and arrange on a baking sheet. Bake on the upper level of a 450° oven 5 minutes, or until delicately browned. Fill as desired and serve hot or at room temperature, depending on the filling. These shells are an excellent substitute for patty shells.

COCKTAIL PUFFS

½ cup water
4 tablespoons butter
¼ teaspoon salt
Dash cayenne pepper
½ cup sifted flour
2 eggs

Bring the water, butter, salt and cayenne pepper to a boil. Add the flour all at once, stirring constantly with a wooden spoon over low heat until a ball of dough is formed and mixture leaves the sides of the pan. Remove from the heat. Add 1 egg at a time, beating until glossy after each addition. Drop by the heaping teaspoon onto a cooky sheet, leaving 1 inch between each. Bake in a preheated 325° oven 20 minutes, or until browned and free from moisture. Cool and split. Makes about 32. Fill with one of the following:

Crab Meat:

1 tablespoon butter
2 tablespoons minced onions
3 tablespoons chopped mushrooms
1 cup finely chopped crab meat
1 tablespoon minced parsley
1 teaspoon salt
⅛ teaspoon Tabasco

Melt the butter in a skillet; sauté the onions and mushrooms 5 minutes. Stir in the crab meat, parsley, salt and Tabasco. Sauté 1 minute. Cool. Fill the puffs.

Caviar:

4 tablespoons cream cheese
½ cup sour cream
1 tablespoon grated onion
½ cup black or red caviar

Soften the cheese and mix with the sour cream until smooth. Fold in the onion and caviar. Fill the puffs.

Guacamole (avocado):

1 avocado
2 tablespoons chopped onions
1 tomato, chopped

2 tablespoons lime or lemon juice
1 teaspoon salt
2 teaspoons chili powder

Scoop out the pulp of the avocado and combine in an electric blender with the onions, tomato, lime juice, salt and chili powder. Run in the blender, or chop until smooth. Taste for seasoning and fill the puffs.

Shrimp-Avocado:

1 avocado
1 cup cooked chopped shrimp

2 tablespoons grated onions
¼ cup Russian dressing

Scoop out the pulp of the avocado; chop coarsely. Combine with the shrimp, onions and Russian dressing. Taste for seasoning and fill the puffs.

Pâté:

Mash 1 8-ounch can pâté, or use any homemade variety. Fill the puffs.

CHEESE-PASTRY SANDWICHES

Pastry:

2 cups sifted flour
¼ teaspoon salt
¼ teaspoon paprika
1 cup ground blanched almonds

⅜ pound (1½ sticks) butter
¾ cup grated cheddar cheese
2 egg yolks

Sift the flour, salt and paprika into a bowl. Mix in the almonds. With the hand work in the butter, cheese and then the egg yolks. Chill 1 hour. Roll out the dough ¼ inch thick between two pieces of wax paper and cut into strips 2 inches long by 1 inch wide, or into 1-inch circles. Arrange

111

on a greased, floured baking sheet and bake in a 375° oven 10 minutes, or until delicately browned. Cool.

Filling:

¼ pound (1 stick) butter
1/3 cup grated cheddar cheese
1/3 cup grated Parmesan cheese
Dash cayenne pepper

Cream the butter, then work in the cheeses and cayenne pepper. Spread between 2 strips or circles, making sandwiches.

Makes about 24.

CHEESE ROLL APPETIZER

2 cups sifted flour
2 teaspoons salt
½ pound butter
1/3 cup sour cream
1 pound pot cheese

2 egg yolks
2 tablespoons chopped dill
2 egg whites
4 tablespoons melted butter

Sift the flour and 1 teaspoon of the salt into a bowl. Work in the butter with the hand. Add 4 tablespoons sour cream, blending until a dough is formed. Chill a few hours or overnight, if possible.

Force the cheese through a sieve. Add the egg yolks, dill, remaining salt and sour cream. Beat the egg whites until stiff but not dry. Fold into the cheese mixture. Divide the dough in half and roll out each half as thin as possible. Brush each half with the melted butter. Spread half the cheese mixture over each and roll up like a jelly roll. Arrange the rolls in a buttered baking pan.

Bake in a preheated 425° oven 30 minutes or until crisp and brown. Cut into 1-inch slices while hot. Serve hot or cold.

Makes about 48 slices.

CHEESE PASTRY SLICES

¼ pound (1 stick) butter
2 cups (½ pound) grated cheddar
  or Swiss cheese

1 cup sifted flour
¼ teaspoon salt
Dash cayenne pepper

Cream together the butter and cheese. Sift in the flour, salt and cayenne pepper, mixing until a ball of dough is formed. Shape into long rolls ¾ inch in diameter. Chill until firm enough to slice. Slice ⅛ inch thick. Arrange on lightly greased baking sheets. Bake in a 400° oven 10 minutes. Cool.

Makes about 5 dozen.

Note: The slices taste best freshly baked. If they are not to be served the same day, keep unbaked portion in the refrigerator a week and bake as needed.

PARMESAN CHEESE PUFFS

¾ cup milk	⅛ teaspoon salt
¼ pound butter	2 eggs
¾ cup sifted flour	1 cup grated Parmesan cheese

Combine the milk and butter in a saucepan. Bring to a boil. Add the flour and salt all at once; cook over low heat, beating constantly with a wooden spoon until mixture leaves the sides of the pan. Remove from heat. Add one egg at a time, beating well after each addition until smooth and glossy. Mix in the cheese.

Drop heaping teaspoonfuls (or use a pastry bag) onto a buttered baking sheet.

Bake in a preheated 400° oven 10 minutes; reduce heat to 325° and continue baking 15 minutes or until browned. Remove from pan immediately. The puffs may be served as they are, or split and filled with any spread.

Makes about 24.

Fillings:

Anchovy:
Mix together ½ cup anchovy paste and ¾ cup heavy cream.

Cheddar Cheese:
Beat together ½ cup grated cheddar cheese, 2 teaspoons prepared mustard and ½ cup heavy cream.

Roquefort Cheese:

Mash ¼ pound Roquefort cheese with ½ cup heavy cream.

Deviled Ham:

Mix together until smooth 1 2¼-ounce can deviled ham, 2 teaspoons grated onions, 1 teaspoon prepared mustard, 2 tablespoons Parmesan cheese and ¼ cup heavy cream.

OLIVES IN CHEESE PASTRY

1 cup sifted flour
½ teaspoon baking powder
½ teaspoon salt
¼ pound butter
1 egg yolk

½ cup milk
1 cup (¼ pound) grated cheddar cheese
24 large pitted black olives

Sift the flour, baking powder and salt into a bowl. Cut in the butter with a pastry blender or 2 knives. Stir in the egg yolk beaten with the milk until a ball of dough is formed. Chill 2 hours.

Roll out the dough ¼ inch thick on a lightly floured surface. Sprinkle with the cheese, fold over and roll out again. Fold over and roll out ¼ inch thick; cut in 2-inch circles. Place an olive in the center and cover with the dough, sealing the edges well. Arrange on a baking sheet. Bake in a preheated 425° oven 12 minutes or until delicately browned. Serve hot.

Makes 24.

PIZZA COCKTAIL BISCUITS

2 cups packaged biscuit mix
1 cup grated Parmesan cheese
1 8-ounce can tomato sauce
½ teaspoon orégano
¾ teaspoon freshly ground black pepper
Sliced sausages or anchovy fillets

Stir together the biscuit mix, cheese, tomato sauce, orégano and pepper. Beat just until blended. Drop by the tablespoon onto an oiled baking sheet. Press a sausage slice or anchovy fillet on each, or make both varieties. Bake in a 450° oven 12 minutes or until browned. Serve hot.

Makes about 36.

BATONS DE FROMAGE (Cheese Pastry Sticks, French Style)

1 cup sifted flour
½ teaspoon salt
Dash of cayenne pepper
¼ pound (1 stick) butter
1 cup grated American or cheddar cheese

Sift the flour, salt and cayenne into a bowl. Cut in the butter and cheese with pastry blender or 2 knives, then form into a ball with the hands. Wrap in foil or wax paper and chill 30 minutes.

On a lightly floured surface roll out the pastry ¼ inch thick. Cut into ½ by 3-inch strips and arrange on a cooky sheet. Bake in a preheated 425° oven 8 minutes or until lightly browned. Serve hot or cold. To keep, store in an air-tight container.

Makes about 36.

CAMEMBERT PASTRY ROUNDS

½ pound Camembert cheese
6 tablespoons soft butter
3 eggs

2 cups sifted flour
½ teaspoon salt
2 dashes cayenne pepper

Buy a soft Camembert cheese, and carefully remove the rind. Mash smooth. Mix in the butter, then 2 of the eggs. Sift the flour, salt and pepper over the cheese mixture, and then with the hand mix it in until a smooth dough is formed. If dough seems too soft, knead in a little more flour. Form into a ball, wrap in foil or wax paper and chill 2 hours.

On a lightly floured surface, roll out the dough ¼ inch thick. Cut into 1½-inch rounds and arrange on lightly greased baking sheets. Brush the tops with the remaining egg beaten with 1 teaspoon water. Chill 10 minutes. Bake in a 350° oven 12 minutes, or until delicately browned. Cool on a cake rack. If desired, the tops of the pastries may be sprinkled with poppy, caraway or sesame seeds before baking.

Makes about 48.

Note: This pastry may also be used for turnovers or barquettes.

SWISS CHEESE IN PASTRY

2¼ cups sifted flour
1 teaspoon salt
¾ cup shortening
6 tablespoons cold water

4 slices Swiss cheese, cut ½ inch thick
1 egg, beaten

Sift together the flour and salt; cut in the shortening until the mixture looks like coarse corn meal. Sprinkle the water over the mixture and mix lightly until all the flour is moistened. Form into a ball and chill 30 minutes.

Cut the cheese into 1½-inch squares. Roll out the dough ⅛ inch thick and cut into 4-inch squares. Place a piece of cheese on each piece of dough and fold over into a triangle. Moisten the edges with a little water and press firmly together. Prick the tops and brush with beaten egg.

Arrange on a baking sheet and bake in a 425° oven 15 minutes, or until browned. Serve hot.

Makes about 18.

ROQUEFORT CHEESE STRUDEL

1 package strudel leaves
¼ pound Roquefort cheese
½ cup heavy cream
1 cup cottage cheese, drained
1 egg yolk
¼ teaspoon salt

¼ teaspoon freshly ground black pepper
2 egg whites, beaten to a froth
½ cup melted butter
Dry bread crumbs

Remove the package of strudel leaves from the refrigerator 4 hours before using. Mash the Roquefort cheese.

Beat together the Roquefort cheese, cream, cottage cheese, egg yolk, salt and pepper. Fold in the egg whites and taste for seasoning.

Spread a large damp towel on a flat surface. Open an envelope of strudel leaves and place one on the cloth (keep the remaining dough covered to prevent drying). Brush the leaf with butter and sprinkle with crumbs. Repeat this procedure with three more layers of leaves, one on top of the other.

Spread the short edge closest to you with the cheese mixture in a strip about 3 inches wide.

Pick up the edge of the towel and roll up the strudel, folding in the sides of the leaves at the same time. Roll onto a greased baking sheet and brush the top with butter.

Bake in a 375° oven 25 minutes, or until golden brown. Slide onto a bread board, cut into 2-inch pieces and serve hot.

Serves 8.

TARTE AU POISSON (Fish Pie, French Style)

Half Recipe Sour Cream Pastry

3 tablespoons butter
¾ cup thinly sliced onions
2½ teaspoons salt
1 cup flaked cooked fish or diced shrimp
3 tomatoes, peeled and sliced
¼ teaspoon freshly ground black pepper
2 eggs
¾ cup heavy cream
⅛ teaspoon cayenne pepper

Line a 9-inch pie plate with pastry and bake in a 400° oven 10 minutes. Cool.

Melt the butter in a skillet; sauté the onions 10 minutes. Season with ½ teaspoon salt. Arrange the fish and tomatoes in the pastry shell; season with 1 teaspoon salt and the black pepper. Spread onions evenly on the tomatoes. Beat together the eggs, cream, cayenne pepper and remaining salt; pour into the pie plate. Bake in a preheated 375° oven 25 minutes or until set and lightly browned. Serve hot, cut in wedges.

Makes about 8 wedges.

CHINESE FRIED PASTRY ROLLS

2 cups sifted flour
2 teaspoons salt
½ cup shortening
1 egg yolk
¼ cup ice water
¼ pound crab meat or cooked clean shrimp
½ cup diced cooked meat or chicken
½ cup sliced mushrooms
4 water chestnuts
¼ cup sliced green onions
½ cup cooked fine noodles
½ teaspoon freshly ground black pepper
½ teaspoon powdered ginger
Vegetable oil for deep frying

Sift together the flour and 1 teaspoon of the salt. Cut in the shortening until the consistency of coarse corn meal. Beat the egg yolk with the water and stir into the flour mixture until a ball of dough is formed. Wrap in foil or wax paper and chill 1 hour.

Chop together the crab meat or shrimp, meat or chicken, mushrooms, water chestnuts, onions, noodles, pepper, ginger and remaining salt.

Roll out the dough and cut into 3-inch circles. Spread some of the filling on one side, turn opposite ends in over the filling, then roll up like a jelly roll. Seal the edges with a little egg white.

Heat the oil to 365° and fry a few rolls at a time, without crowding the pan, 8 minutes or until browned. Drain and keep hot while preparing the balance.

Makes about 20.

BOUCHÉES NEPTUNE (French Seafood Puffs)

¼ pound (1 stick) butter
1 cup bottled clam juice
1 cup sifted flour
3 eggs

1/3 cup mayonnaise
2 teaspoons curry powder
1 cup cooked lobster, shrimp or crab meat, chopped

Combine the butter and clam juice in a saucepan. Bring to a boil, and when butter melts, add the flour all at once, beating with a wooden spoon until the mixture leaves the sides of the pan. Remove from the heat and add 1 egg at a time, beating until smooth and shiny after each addition.

Force the mixture through a pastry tube onto a baking sheet into walnut-sized balls, or shape with two spoons. Bake in a 425° oven 5 minutes. Reduce heat to 350° and bake 10 minutes longer, or until puffs are browned and free of moisture. Cool.

Mix the mayonnaise with the curry powder, then fold in the seafood. Taste for seasoning. Make a slit on the side of each puff and fill with about a teaspoon of the seafood mixture.

Makes about 36.

Note: The filled puffs may also be dipped in batter and fried in 375° deep fat for 1 minute.

EMPANADITAS (Fried Stuffed Cocktail Pies, Argentine Style)

1½ cups sifted flour
½ teaspoon salt
1½ teaspoons baking powder
2 tablespoons butter
3 egg yolks, beaten
¼ cup ice water (about)

1 cup cottage cheese
¼ cup chopped black olives
⅛ teaspoon cayenne pepper
2 egg whites, beaten stiff
Vegetable oil for deep frying

Sift the flour, salt and baking powder into a bowl. Cut in the butter with a pastry blender or two knives. Add the egg yolks, tossing lightly with a fork. Add enough ice water to make a soft dough. Roll out ⅛ inch thick on a lightly floured board. Cut into 2-inch circles with a cooky cutter.

Drain all the liquid from the cheese. Mix together the cheese, olives and cayenne pepper. Fold in the egg whites. Place a teaspoon of the cheese mixture on each circle and cover with another circle, sealing the edges well.

Heat the fat to 375° and drop the pies into it. Fry until lightly browned. Drain. Serve hot.

Makes about 24.

EMPADINHAS DE CAMARÃOS (Brazilian Shrimp Pastries)

1½ cups sifted flour
2 teaspoons salt
¾ cup shortening
1 egg, beaten
¼ cup ice water
2 tablespoons olive oil
¾ cup chopped onions
5 tomatoes, peeled and chopped or
  1½ cups canned tomatoes, drained

1½ cups cooked, coarsely chopped
  shrimp
½ teaspoon freshly ground black
  pepper
1 hard-cooked egg, chopped
¼ cup chopped ripe olives
3 tablespoons chopped parsley

Sift the flour and 1 teaspoon salt into a bowl. Cut in the shortening with a pastry blender or two knives until consistency of coarse sand. Add the egg and water, tossing lightly until dough forms a ball. Wrap in wax paper and chill 2 hours.

Heat the oil in a skillet and sauté the onions 10 minutes.

Add the tomatoes and cook over low heat 10 minutes. Mix in the shrimp, pepper and remaining salt. Cook over low heat 10 minutes. Remove from heat and mix in the chopped egg, olives and parsley. Taste for seasoning. Cool 15 minutes.

Roll out the dough ¼ inch thick on a lightly floured board. Cut into 5-inch circles. Place 1 tablespoon shrimp mixture in the center of each circle and fold over the dough, sealing the edges with a little water. Arrange on a baking sheet and bake in a 400° oven 20 minutes. Serve hot.

Makes about 24.

EMPANADITAS (Spanish Meat Pastries)

Pastry:

1½ cups sifted flour	1 egg, beaten
¾ teaspoon salt	3 tablespoons ice water
¾ cup shortening	

Sift the flour and salt into a bowl; cut in the shortening. Add the egg and water, tossing with a fork until a ball of dough is formed. Chill several hours or overnight.

Filling:

3 tablespoons olive oil	2 teaspoons A.1. Sauce
¾ cup chopped onions	1 teaspoon salt
½ cup chopped green pepper	⅛ teaspoon cayenne pepper
½ cup chopped tomato	½ cup chopped stuffed green olives
½ pound ground beef	2 hard-cooked eggs, chopped

Heat the oil in a skillet; sauté the onions 5 minutes. Add the green pepper and tomato; sauté 5 minutes. Add the meat, A.1. Sauce, salt and cayenne pepper; cook over low heat 10 minutes, stirring frequently. Cool, then mix in the olives and eggs; taste for seasoning.

Roll out the dough as thin as possible on a lightly floured surface. Cut into 4-inch circles. Place a tablespoon of the meat mixture on each. Fold over the dough into a half-moon and seal edges with a little water. Arrange on a baking pan.

Bake in a preheated 400° oven 15 minutes or until browned.
Serve hot.

Makes about 2 dozen.

SCHINKEN-GIPFELI (Swiss Ham Crescents)

2 cups chopped cooked ham	Puff Paste recipe
1/3 cup heavy cream	1 egg yolk
2 teaspoons prepared mustard	

Mix together the ham, cream and mustard. Roll out the
pastry very thin and cut into triangles 5 inches long at the
wide part. Put a tablespoon of filling on each and roll up
from the wide side. Turn ends in to form a crescent. Arrange on baking sheets and chill 20 minutes. Brush tops with
the egg yolk beaten with 1 teaspoon water. Bake in a 400°
oven 15 minutes or until browned. Serve hot or at room
temperature.

Makes about 32.

PIROSHKI (Russian Meat Pastries)

1 cup flour	1/4 pound livers
1 teaspoon salt	1 pound mushrooms sliced
3/8 pound (1½ sticks) butter	1/2 teaspoon freshly ground black
3 tablespoons sour cream	pepper

Sift the flour and ½ teaspoon salt into a bowl. Work in 1
stick of the butter with the hand until well blended. Mix in
sour cream until smooth. Wrap in wax paper and chill overnight or at least 2 hours.

Melt the remaining butter in a skillet and sauté the livers,
mushrooms, pepper and remaining salt for 10 minutes over
low heat. Chop fine and cool. Roll out chilled dough ⅛ inch
thick on a lightly floured board and cut into 3-inch rounds
with a cooky cutter. Place a heaping teaspoon of liver filling
on each and fold over, sealing the edges with a little water.
Arrange on a baking sheet and bake in a 375° oven 15 minutes or until delicately browned. Serve hot.

Makes about 20.

PETITS PÂTES STRASBOURGEOISE (Strasbourg Stuffed Shells)

Puff Paste recipe
1 8-ounce can purée de foie gras
2 truffles, cut in very thin strips

1 egg white
1 egg yolk
2 tablespoons cream

Roll out the puff paste ⅛ inch thick. Cut into 1½-inch rounds. Place a teaspoon of the foie gras on half the rounds. Place a piece of truffle over the foie gras. Brush edges with egg white and cover with the remaining rounds, pressing the edges together. Arrange on baking sheets and brush with the egg yolk beaten with the cream. Chill 15 minutes, then bake in a 425° oven 12 minutes or until delicately browned. Serve hot or cold.

Makes about 48.

SAMBOUSIKS (Curried Pastries, Near East Style)

1¼ cups sifted flour
1 teaspoon salt
¾ cup (1½ sticks) butter
3 tablespoons ice water

¾ cup milk, scalded
1 tablespoon curry powder
1½ cups chopped beef or chicken

Sift all but 1 teaspoon of the flour and ½ teaspoon salt into a bowl. Cut in the butter (reserving 1 tablespoon) with a pastry blender or two knives. Gradually add the ice water, tossing lightly until a dough is formed. Chill 15 minutes, then roll out on a lightly floured board. Fold dough in half and then in quarters. Roll out again and fold over into thirds. Wrap in wax paper and chill 1 hour.

Melt the reserved 1 tablespoon butter in a saucepan; blend in the reserved tablespoon flour. Gradually add the milk, stirring to the boiling point. Mix in the curry powder and remaining salt and cook over low heat 5 minutes. Stir in the meat or chicken. Taste for seasoning. Cool.

Roll out the dough ⅛ inch thick on a lightly floured board and cut into 3-inch circles. Place a tablespoon of the meat mixture in the center of each round, fold over dough and seal edges with a little egg white or water. Arrange on a baking sheet and bake in a preheated 375° oven 15 minutes or until browned. Serve hot.

Makes about 24.

PASTELITOS DE PUERCO (Pork Pastries, Spanish Style)

2 cups sifted flour
¾ cup (1½ sticks) butter
2/3 cup orange juice
3 tablespoons olive oil
2 tablespoons chopped onions
2 tablespoons chopped green pepper
1/3 clove garlic, minced

¾ pound ground pork
1 hard-cooked egg, mashed
¼ cup chopped green olives
¼ cup seedless raisins
1½ teaspoons salt
¼ teaspoon freshly ground black pepper

Sift the flour into a bowl; cut in the butter with a pastry blender or two knives. Stir in the orange juice until a ball of dough is formed. Chill while preparing the pork.

Heat the oil in a skillet; sauté the onions, green pepper, garlic, and pork until no pink remains in the pork. Mix in the egg, olives, raisins, salt, and pepper. Cook 5 minutes; taste for seasoning and cool.

Roll out the dough as thin as possible; cut into 2-inch circles. Place a tablespoon of the pork mixture on half the circles and cover with the remaining circles. Seal the edges with a little water. Arrange on a baking sheet. Brush tops with cream or beaten egg yolks. Bake in a preheated 425° oven 15 minutes or until browned. Serve hot.

Makes about 18.

SAMOSAS (Indian Pastries)

Pastry:

2 cups sifted flour
1 teaspoon salt
¼ cup melted butter
¼ cup yogurt

Sift the flour and salt into a bowl. Stir in the butter, then the yogurt. Turn out onto a lightly floured surface and knead until a dough is formed. Cover with a cloth and let stand while preparing the filling.

123

Filling:

2 tablespoons butter
½ cup chopped onions
1 clove garlic, minced
½ pound ground beef
½ cup chopped tomato
¾ teaspoon salt

¼ teaspoon freshly ground black pepper
1 tablespoon curry powder
2 teaspoons lemon juice
Vegetable oil for deep frying

Melt the butter in a skillet; sauté the onions and garlic 5 minutes. Add the meat; cook over high heat 5 minutes, stirring frequently. Add the tomato, salt, pepper, curry powder and lemon juice. Cook over medium heat 5 minutes or until all the liquid is absorbed, stirring frequently. Cool.

Roll out the dough as thin as possible and cut into 3-inch circles. Place a heaping teaspoon of the filling on each and fold over into a half-moon, sealing the edges with a little water.

Heat the oil to 370°. Fry a few pastries at a time until browned and crisp. Drain. Keep hot while preparing the balance.

Makes about 24.

PISSALADIERA NICOISE (Onion Appetizer, Nice Style)

1 package hot roll mix
1⅛ cups olive oil
3 pounds onions, thinly sliced
2 cloves garlic, minced
1¼ teaspoons salt

½ teaspoon freshly ground black pepper
1 can anchovy fillets
Pitted black olives

Prepare the hot roll mix as package directs, adding ⅛ cup of the oil as you knead; roll it out very thin and line an 11 by 17-inch baking pan with the dough.

Heat the remaining oil in a skillet; sauté the onions, garlic, salt and pepper 25 minutes, mixing frequently. Drain and cool. Spread onion mixture evenly over dough and arrange the anchovy fillets in a lattice design, making 2-inch squares. Put a black olive in center of each square. Bake in a preheated 350° oven 30 minutes. Cut into squares and serve hot.

Makes about 45 squares.

TARTE AUX OIGNONS (French Onion-Anchovy Tart)

¼ cup olive oil
3 cups thinly sliced onions
1 teaspoon salt
½ teaspoon black pepper

11-inch pastry-lined pie plate
2 tomatoes, thinly sliced
1 can anchovy fillets
Pitted black olives

Heat the oil in a skillet; mix in the onions. Cover and cook over low heat 20 minutes, or until soft and yellow but not browned. Season with the salt and pepper. Cool. Spread in the lined pie plate. Arrange the tomatoes over the onions, then the anchovies in a crisscross pattern. Arrange as many olives as you like on the top. Bake in a preheated 400° oven 25 minutes. Cut into wedges.

Makes 10 wedges.

GREEK SPINACH-FETA STRUDEL

1 package strudel leaves
1 pound fresh spinach or 1 package frozen, thawed
3 tablespoons olive oil
½ pound sweet butter
1 cup finely chopped onions
½ cup chopped green onions, green part and all
¼ pound feta cheese, chopped, or cottage cheese

¼ cup fresh dill, chopped, or 1 tablespoon dried dill
¼ cup chopped parsley
2 eggs, beaten
½ teaspoon salt
¼ teaspoon freshly ground black pepper

Remove the package of strudel leaves from the refrigerator 4 hours before using.

Wash the spinach in several changes of water. Dry it and cut into 2-inch lengths. Or drain the frozen spinach. Cook it in the oil 3 minutes. Drain and remove spinach. In the same pan, melt 4 tablespoons of butter. Sauté the onions 10 minutes.

Mix together the sautéed onions, green onions, cheese, dill and parsley. Blend in the eggs, then the spinach, salt and pepper. Taste for seasoning.

Melt the remaining butter.

Butter a square 8 by 8 by 2-inch pan. Cut two strudel leaves into 6 squares each by cutting in half lengthwise and

125

in thirds across (keep the remaining strudel leaves covered to prevent drying).

Place one of the squares in the prepared pan and brush with melted butter. Repeat with the remaining eleven strudel squares, placing each on top of the last. Spread with the spinach-cheese filling and cover with 12 more squares, brushing each with butter.

With a sharp knife, cut through the top to mark it into 2-inch squares. Bake in a 350° oven 40 minutes, or until brown and very puffy. Cut into squares and serve hot as a first course.

Makes 16 squares.

EGG AND SPINACH PIE

Pastry for 1-crust pie
1 package frozen spinach, cooked and drained
4 eggs
¾ teaspoon salt
⅛ teaspoon nutmeg
1 cup sour cream
¾ cup soft bread crumbs
2 tablespoons melted butter
2 tablespoons grated cheese

Roll out the pastry ⅛ inch thick and fit loosely into an 8-inch pie plate. Prick the bottom and sides well with a fork and bake on the lower shelf of a 450° oven 8 minutes, or until set but not brown. Remove from oven; reduce heat to 350°.

Chop the drained spinach coarsely. Spread over the pastry. Beat together the eggs, salt, nutmeg and sour cream. Pour over the spinach.

Toss the crumbs with the butter and cheese and sprinkle over the top. Return pie to the oven and bake 20 minutes or until the custard is set. Serve hot, cut into wedges.

Makes about 8 wedges.

HORS D'OEUVRE NUT SLICES

1-1/3 cups sifted flour
1 teaspoon salt
¼ pound (1 stick) soft butter
1 whole raw egg
2 hard-cooked egg yolks, mashed
1 raw egg yolk
1 tablespoon milk
¾ cup ground almonds, filberts, walnuts or Brazil nuts
2 teaspoons coarse salt
⅛ teaspoon nutmeg

Sift the flour and salt into a bowl. Make a well in the center and into it put the butter, raw egg and hard-cooked egg yolks. With the fingers, work the ingredients in the well to a paste, then work in the flour until a ball of dough is formed. Wrap in wax paper and chill 3 hours or overnight. Form the dough into long rolls ¾ inch in diameter. Chill again until firm. With a sharp knife, cut into slices ¼ inch thick. Arrange on baking sheets. Brush tops with the egg yolk beaten with the milk and sprinkle heavily with a mixture of the nuts, salt and nutmeg. Bake in a 350° oven 12 minutes or until lightly browned.

Makes about 3 dozen.

Variation: Nut Wheels

Roll out half the chilled pastry at a time into an oblong ¼ inch thick. Brush tops with the egg yolks beaten with the milk. Sprinkle with a mixture of the nuts, salt and nutmeg. Press in gently with a rolling pin, then roll up like a jelly roll, making a long roll. Chill 1 hour, cut into slices ¼ inch thick, arrange flat on a baking sheet and bake as directed.

QUICHES

WITHIN the last few years quiches have become one of the most popular of all hors d'oeuvres. These unsweetened custard pies deserve their popularity, as the light, fluffy filling in a flaky pastry shell is perfect as an appetizer. Most people are familiar with quiche Lorraine, a bacon-custard tart, but there are many variations. These are always prepared with the custard mixture but the other ingredients range from onions or cheese to different kinds of seafood or smoked fish. The traditional quiche is baked in a 9-inch round pan, and the finished pie is cut into wedges. You can of course, make individual small-sized tarts. The amounts specified in the following recipes are sufficient for eight 3-inch tarts, but

127

reduce the baking time of the filled tarts by 10 minutes. Baked quiches may be frozen satisfactorily, and then heated in the oven before serving.

The quiche is native to France, and is an outstanding example of the cuisine régionale, for various types of quiche originated in different provinces of France. Quiche Lorraine began in historic old Lorraine, situated on France's border with Germany. The quiche au Roquefort comes from the tiny town of Roquefort in southwestern France, and the quiche aux fruits de mer probably originated in Brittany, fronting on the Atlantic Ocean, where seafood is always available.

QUICHES (Custard Pastry Appetizer)

All quiches are prepared in the same manner, but with different ingredients in the custard mixture.

Pastry:

1½ cups sifted flour
½ teaspoon salt
3 tablespoons vegetable shortening

6 tablespoons butter
3 tablespoons ice water

Sift the flour and salt into a bowl. With the fingers, work in the shortening and the butter, broken into small pieces, until the mixture looks like coarse corn meal. Mix in the water with the fingers until a dough is formed. Knead very lightly and form the dough into a ball. Wrap in wax paper or foil and chill in the refrigerator overnight, if possible, or at least 2 hours; or 1 hour in the freezer.

On a lightly floured surface, roll out the dough ⅛ inch thick and fit into a lightly greased 9-inch pie plate, flan ring or straight-sided cake pan. Using a small piece of dough dipped in flour, gently press the pastry into the pan. Flute the edge and prick the bottom with a fork in several places. Place a slightly smaller pan in the pastry shell to keep it from shrinking or put a piece of wax paper in it and fill with beans or rice.

Bake in a 400° oven 10 minutes, remove the weight and bake 1 minute longer. Cool on a cake rack.

128

QUICHE LORRAINE (Bacon Tart)

6 slices bacon
4 eggs
½ teaspoon salt
Dash white pepper

Dash nutmeg
2 cups heavy cream
2 tablespoons butter

Brown the bacon in a skillet; drain and arrange in the pastry shell, pressing down gently. Beat together the eggs, salt, pepper and nutmeg, then beat in the cream. Slowly pour into the shell and dot with the butter. Bake in a 375° oven in the middle level 25 minutes or until puffed and browned and a knife inserted in the center comes out clean. Cut into wedges.

QUICHE AU FROMAGE (Cheese Tart)

2 cups (½ pound) grated Swiss or
  Gruyère cheese
1 tablespoon flour
4 eggs

¼ teaspoon salt
Dash nutmeg
2 cups light cream
2 tablespoons butter

Toss the cheese with the flour and spread in the pastry shell. Beat the eggs, salt and nutmeg, then beat in the cream; slowly pour into the shell. Dot with the butter. Bake in a 375° oven on the middle level 25 minutes or until a knife inserted in the center comes out clean. Cut into wedges.

QUICHE AU ROQUEFORT (Roquefort Tart)

¼ pound Roquefort cheese
½ pound cream cheese
3 tablespoons soft butter
¼ cup heavy cream

3 eggs
½ teaspoon salt
Dash cayenne pepper
1 tablespoon minced parsley

Beat together the Roquefort cheese, cream cheese, butter and cream until smooth, then beat in 1 egg at a time. If there are any lumps, force the mixture through a sieve. Mix in the salt, cayenne pepper and parsley. Turn into the pastry shell. Bake in a 375° oven 25 minutes, or until puffed and browned. Cut into wedges.

QUICHE AUX FRUITS DE MER (Seafood Tart)

3 tablespoons butter
3 tablespoons minced green onions
1½ cups cooked diced shrimp,
    lobster or flaked crab meat
1 tablespoon tomato paste
¾ teaspoon salt
Dash cayenne pepper

3 tablespoons sweet sherry
4 eggs
1½ cups heavy cream
¼ teaspoon white pepper
¼ cup grated Swiss or Gruyère
    cheese

Melt the butter in a skillet; sauté the green onions 2 minutes. Add the seafood; cook 2 minutes, stirring almost constantly. Mix in the tomato paste, half the salt, the cayenne pepper and sherry. Bring to a boil and cook over high heat 1 minute. Cool 10 minutes.

Beat the eggs, then beat in the cream, pepper and remaining salt. Stir in the seafood mixture. Turn into the pastry shell and sprinkle with the cheese. Bake in a 375° oven 25 minutes or until a knife inserted in the center comes out clean. Cut into wedges.

QUICHE AUX CHAMPIGNONS (Mushroom Tart)

5 tablespoons butter
3 tablespoons minced green onions
1¼ pounds mushrooms, sliced
1½ teaspoons salt
¼ teaspoon white pepper
2 tablespoons madeira or sweet sherry

4 eggs
2 cups heavy cream
¼ cup grated Swiss or Gruyère
    cheese

Melt 3 tablespoons of the butter in a saucepan; sauté the green onions 1 minute. Add the mushrooms, 1 teaspoon of the salt, the pepper and wine. Cover and cook over medium heat 5 minutes. Remove cover and cook over high heat until the liquid is evaporated and mushrooms slightly browned. Cool 10 minutes.

Beat the eggs with the remaining salt, then beat in the cream. Stir in the mushrooms. Turn into the pastry shell; sprinkle with the cheese and dot with the remaining butter.

Bake in a 375° oven 25 minutes or until a knife inserted in the center comes out clean. Cut into wedges.

QUICHE AUX TOMATES (Tomato Tart)

5 tablespoons olive oil	½ teaspoon orégano
½ cup minced onions	2 whole eggs
2 pounds tomatoes, peeled and chopped	3 egg yolks
1 clove garlic, minced	¼ cup minced anchovies
½ teaspoon salt	¼ cup chopped parsley
¼ teaspoon freshly ground black pepper	Dash cayenne pepper
	¼ cup grated Parmesan cheese
	2 tablespoons butter

Heat 3 tablespoons of the oil in a skillet; sauté the onions 5 minutes, stirring frequently. Add the tomatoes, garlic, salt, pepper and orégano. Bring to a boil and cook over low heat 15 minutes, or until liquid is evaporated. Stir occasionally. Cool 10 minutes.

Beat the egg and egg yolks, then beat in the anchovies, parsley, cayenne pepper and remaining oil. Mix in the tomatoes; turn into pastry shell. Sprinkle with the cheese and dot with the butter. Bake in a 375° oven 25 minutes or until puffed and browned. Cut into wedges.

QUICHE AUX OIGNONS (Onion Tart)

2 pounds onions	1½ teaspoons salt
3 tablespoons butter	4 eggs
½ teaspoon sugar	1½ cups sour cream
½ teaspoon freshly ground black pepper	⅛ teaspoon nutmeg
	Dash cayenne pepper

Peel the onions and slice paper-thin. Melt the butter in a skillet; add the onions, sugar, pepper and 1 teaspoon of the salt. Sauté until soft and yellow, stirring frequently. Cool 20 minutes. Taste for seasoning.

Beat together the eggs, sour cream, nutmeg, cayenne and remaining salt. Stir in the onions. Turn into the pastry shell. Bake in a 350° oven 35 minutes or until puffed and browned. Cut into wedges.

QUICHE AUX OIGNONS ET ANCHOIS (Onion-Anchovy Tart)

4 tablespoons butter
1½ cups chopped onions
1 teaspoon salt
10 anchovy fillets
4 eggs

1¾ cups heavy cream
¼ teaspoon white pepper
¼ cup grated Swiss or Gruyère cheese

Melt 3 tablespoons of the butter in a skillet. Add the onions and ½ teaspoon of the salt; sauté 10 minutes, stirring frequently. Cool.

Spread half the onions in the pastry shell; arrange the anchovies over them and cover with the remaining onions.

Beat the eggs, then beat in the cream, pepper and remaining salt. Pour into the pastry shell. Sprinkle with the cheese and dot with the remaining butter. Bake in a 375° oven 30 minutes or until puffed and browned. Cut into wedges.

QUICHE AUX OIGNONS ET FROMAGE (Onion Tart with Cheese)

2 tablespoons vegetable oil
4 tablespoons butter
7 cups (2 pounds) chopped onions
1 teaspoon sugar
1½ teaspoons salt
1 tablespoon flour

3 eggs
1 cup heavy cream
¼ teaspoon white pepper
Dash nutmeg
½ cup grated Swiss or Gruyère cheese

Heat the oil and 3 tablespoons of the butter in a large skillet. Add the onions, sugar and ½ teaspoon salt. Cook over low heat, stirring occasionally until onions are soft and yellow. Blend in the flour and cook 5 minutes. Cool 10 minutes.

Beat the eggs, then beat in the cream, then the pepper, nutmeg and remaining salt. Blend in half the cheese, and the onions. Turn into the pastry shell, sprinkle with the remaining cheese and dot with the remaining butter. Bake in a 375° oven 25 minutes or until puffed and browned. Cut into wedges.

QUICHE AU HOMARD (Lobster Tart)

½ pound cooked lobster meat, diced
1 teaspoon salt
¼ teaspoon freshly ground black pepper
2 tablespoons dry sherry

2 tablespoons minced parsley
5 eggs
2 cups light cream
Dash cayenne pepper

Mix together the lobster, salt, pepper, sherry and parsley. Taste for seasoning. Spread on the bottom of the pastry shell. Beat together the eggs, cream and cayenne pepper; pour over the lobster. Bake in a 375° oven 30 minutes or until puffed and browned. Let stand 10 minutes and cut into wedges.

QUICHE AUX CREVETTES (Shrimp-Custard Pie)

1 pound raw shrimp, shelled and deveined
3 tablespoons vegetable oil
¾ cup thinly sliced onions
¼ pound mushrooms, sliced
1¾ teaspoons salt
¼ teaspoon freshly ground black pepper

½ cup sliced pimiento-stuffed olives
5 eggs
2 cups light cream
Dash nutmeg
½ cup grated Swiss cheese

Wash, drain and dry the shrimp. Heat the oil in a skillet; sauté the shrimp, onions and mushrooms 5 minutes or until shrimp turn pink. If there is any mushroom liquid left at this time, turn up the heat to dry. Season with ¾ teaspoon salt and half the pepper. Cool 10 minutes.

Spread the shrimp mixture in the pie shell. Sprinkle with the olives. Beat together the eggs, cream, nutmeg and remaining salt and pepper. Pour into the shell. Bake in a 375° oven 20 minutes. Quickly sprinkle the cheese on top and bake 10 minutes longer, or until custard is firm. Cut into wedges.

CLAM QUICHE

1 10½-ounce can minced clams
2 tablespoons butter
¼ cup minced onions
1¼ cups heavy cream (about)
4 eggs

½ teaspoon salt
¼ teaspoon freshly ground black pepper
6 slices crisp bacon, crumbled

Drain the clams, reserving the juice. Melt the butter in a skillet; sauté the onions until soft, but not browned. Measure the clam juice, and add enough cream to make 2 cups liquid.

Beat the eggs, stir in the clam-juice mixture, salt and pepper. Spread the pie shell with the clams, onions and bacon. Slowly pour the custard mixture over it. Bake in a preheated 375° oven 30 minutes, or until lightly browned and a knife inserted in the center comes out clean. Cut in wedges.

QUICHE AU SAUMON FUMÉ (Smoked Salmon Tart)

¼ pound sliced smoked salmon
4 eggs
2 egg yolks
¾ teaspoon salt
¼ teaspoon white pepper
2 cups heavy cream
2 tablespoons butter

Cut each slice of salmon in thirds crosswise. Beat together the eggs, egg yolks, salt and pepper. Beat in the cream. Pour two thirds of the mixture into the pastry shell. Arrange the salmon on it, then slowly pour the remaining egg mixture over the salmon. Dot with the butter. Bake in a 375° oven 25 minutes, or until a knife inserted in the center comes out clean. Cut into wedges.

QUICHE AUX POIREAUX (Leek Tart)

4 cups sliced leeks (white part only)
5 tablespoons butter
½ cup water
1½ teaspoons salt
4 eggs
1¾ cups heavy cream
⅛ teaspoon white pepper
Dash nutmeg
¼ cup grated Swiss or Gruyère cheese

In a saucepan, combine the leeks, 4 tablespoons of the butter, the water and 1 teaspoon of the salt. Cover, bring to a boil and cook over medium heat 15 minutes, or until all the liquid is evaporated and leeks tender. Cool 10 minutes.

Beat the eggs, then beat in the cream, pepper, nutmeg and remaining salt. Mix in the leeks. Turn into the pastry shell. Sprinkle with the cheese and dot with the remaining butter. Bake in a 375° oven 25 minutes or until puffed and browned. Cut into wedges.

QUICHE AUX EPINARDS (Spinach-Quiche)

3 tablespoons butter	¼ teaspoon white pepper
3 tablespoons minced onions	4 eggs
1½ cups chopped cooked spinach	2 cups heavy cream
⅛ teaspoon nutmeg	¼ cup grated Swiss cheese
1 teaspoon salt	

Melt 2 tablespoons butter in a skillet; sauté the onions 3 minutes. Add the spinach; cook until dry, stirring almost constantly. Mix in the nutmeg, ½ teaspoon salt and ⅛ teaspoon pepper. Cool 10 minutes.

Beat the eggs; mix in the cream, and remaining salt and pepper. Mix in the spinach. Pour into the pastry shell; sprinkle with the cheese and dot with the remaining butter. Bake in a preheated 375° oven 30 minutes, or until a knife inserted in the center comes out clean. Cut in wedges.

QUICHE AU FROMAGE BLANC (Cream Cheese-Ham Tart)

½ pound softened cream cheese	¼ teaspoon freshly ground black
1 whole egg	pepper
3 egg yolks	3 thin slices boiled ham, lightly
½ cup heavy cream	browned
½ teaspoon salt	

Beat the cream cheese, egg and egg yolks very smooth in an electric blender, electric mixer or with a rotary beater. Beat in the cream, salt and pepper. It is important that the mixture be completely without lumps, so strain, if necessary.

Arrange the ham on the bottom of the pie shell. Slowly pour the cheese mixture over it. Bake in a preheated 375° oven 25 minutes or until lightly browned and a knife inserted in the center comes out clean. Cut in wedges.

CHEESE

ALMOST everyone likes cheese, and cheese hors d'oeuvres are very easy to prepare. An assortment of sharp or spicy cheeses is also acceptable, but never include a mild or sweet cheese such as Crème Danica or Boursin in the assortment. Cheese dips, and spreads in particular can be prepared a few days in advance. In many cases the flavor is improved, as the cheese has a chance to absorb the other flavors. It is also possible to keep a crock of cheese mixture in the refrigerator as a stand-by for unexpected guests.

When recipes require grated cheese, there are special little graters available to simplify the process. Smooth, creamy mixtures may be prepared in an electric blender. Thinly sliced dark or French bread, crisp crackers, or Scandinavian-type crisp flat breads are all ideal with cheese mixtures.

Every country in Europe makes cheese. Each has its special distinction, each gives that special something to the local cuisine that makes it different from any other. Italy's mozzarella, which has become so popular with Americans, makes an outstanding appetizer, mozzarella milanese, a tasty fried cheese stick. France's Camembert and Brie make delightfully different cheese balls, boulettes de fromage. Belgium makes cheese squares, fondue bruxelloise, which are quite delicious. In Switzerland one finds an exceptional type of appetizer biscuit, sablés suisse.

MOZZARELLA MILANESE (Italian Cheese Sticks)

1 pound mozzarella cheese	½ cup dry bread crumbs
½ cup flour	1½ cups vegetable oil
2 eggs, beaten	

Slice the cheese ¼ inch thick, then cut into sticks 4 inches long by ½ inch wide. Roll in the flour, then dip in the eggs and finally in the bread crumbs, coating them well.

136

Heat the oil in a skillet until it bubbles. Fry a few sticks at a time until browned. Drain and serve hot.

Makes about 16.

DÉLICES D'EMMENTAL (Fried Cheese Sticks)

4 tablespoons butter
1-1/3 cups sifted flour
½ cup dry white wine
1 cup milk
¾ teaspoon salt
Dash cayenne pepper
2 cups (½ pound) grated Gruyère
  or Swiss cheese

3 egg yolks, beaten
1 egg
¼ cup light cream
1 tablespoon olive oil
¾ cup dry bread crumbs
1 cup vegetable oil

Melt the butter in a saucepan; blend in ⅓ cup of the flour. Gradually add the wine and milk, stirring steadily to the boiling point. Stir in the salt and cayenne pepper; cook over low heat 10 minutes, stirring frequently. Remove from the heat and mix in the cheese until melted. Beat in the egg yolks.

Turn into a buttered oblong dish to a depth of ½ inch. Cover with foil or wax paper and chill. Cut into strips about 2 inches long and ½ inch wide. Beat the egg with the cream and olive oil. Dip the sticks in the remaining flour, then the egg mixture, and finally the bread crumbs, coating them thoroughly.

Heat the vegetable oil in a skillet until it bubbles. Fry the sticks in it until browned on all sides. Drain. Don't crowd the pan, and keep oil very hot, or the sticks will melt.

Makes about 32.

BEIGNETS AU FROMAGE (French Cheese Puffs)

¾ cup flour
¼ teaspoon salt
1 egg, beaten
1 tablespoon vegetable oil
½ cup beer

1 egg white, beaten stiff
1 pound unsliced Gruyère or Swiss
  cheese cut into ½-inch cubes
Vegetable oil for deep frying

Sift together ½ cup of the flour and the salt; stir in the egg and oil. Add the beer gradually, stirring until the mixture is smooth. Let stand 1 hour. Fold in the egg white.

137

Toss the cubes of cheese with the remaining flour, then dip into the batter. Heat the oil to 370°. Drop each cube into the fat. (Don't crowd pan.) Fry until browned. Drain on paper towels and serve hot.

Makes about 30.

FONDUE BRUXELLOISE (Fried Cheese Squares, Brussels Fashion)

4 tablespoons butter	⅛ teaspoon freshly ground black
6 tablespoons flour	pepper
1½ cups milk, scalded	3 egg yolks, beaten
2 cups (½ pound) grated Gruyère	½ cup flour
or Swiss cheese	1 egg
1 cup grated Parmesan cheese	½ cup dry bread crumbs
½ teaspoon salt	Vegetable oil for deep frying

Melt the butter in a saucepan; blend in the flour. Add the milk all at once, stirring with a wire whisk. Add the cheeses, salt and pepper; cook, stirring constantly, until the cheese melts. Taste for seasoning and cool. Beat in the egg yolks. Pour the mixture into a buttered 9-inch-square pan. Chill overnight.

Cut into 2-inch squares or diamonds. Dip in the flour, then in the egg beaten with a little water and finally in the bread crumbs. Let dry in the refrigerator 1 hour.

Heat the oil to 390° and fry a few at a time until browned, about 1 minute. Drain on paper towels. Serve at once. Garnish with fried parsley, if desired.

Serves 10.

CRUMBLED CHEESE

Remove the rind of a Camembert, Brie or similar cheese. Cut in small pie-shaped wedges and coat each wedge in ground toasted almonds. Chill. If you prefer, the whole cheese may be rolled in the nuts, then cut into wedges, but the individual wedges are easier to handle.

PARMESAN CHEESE BALLS

3 eggs
1½ cups grated Parmesan cheese
¼ teaspoon salt
¼ teaspoon freshly ground pepper
¼ teaspoon basil

1 tablespoon chopped parsley
1 cup dry bread crumbs
½ cup sifted flour
2 cups vegetable oil

Beat 2 eggs in a bowl. Add the cheese, salt, pepper, basil and parsley, and just enough of the bread crumbs to make a firm mixture. Shape into walnut-sized balls. Beat the remaining egg and dip the balls in it. Roll in the flour, coating them well. Heat oil in a skillet until it bubbles and fry the balls in it until browned on all sides.

Makes about 36.

ROQUEFORT CHEESE BALLS

½ pound Roquefort
¼ pound butter
¼ pound cream cheese
2 tablespoons cognac

1 teaspoon dry mustard
½ cup minced parsley
¼ cup minced chives

Mix together until very smooth the Roquefort, butter, cream cheese, cognac and mustard. Shape into hazelnut-sized balls and roll in the parsley mixed with the chives. Chill and pierce with cocktail picks.

Makes about 60.

FRENCH CHEESE BALLS

½ pound Roquefort cheese
5 tablespoons soft butter
1 tablespoon minced chives or green onion tops

1 teaspoon A.1. Sauce
Dash cayenne pepper
2/3 cup toasted ground blanched almonds

Mash the cheese and butter, then beat until smooth. Blend in the chives, A.1. Sauce and cayenne pepper. Shape into ½-inch balls. Roll in the almonds until well coated. Chill. Pierce with cocktail picks. Makes about 36.

139

BOULETTES DE FROMAGE (Cheese Balls, Provincial Fashion)

8 ounces Camembert or Brie cheese
1 cup dry white wine
½ pound (2 sticks) softened butter

1 cup ground blanched almonds
Toasted blanched almonds

Carefully remove the rind of the cheese. Marinate the trimmed cheese in the wine overnight, turning it several times. Drain. Force the cheese through a food mill or mash smooth. Beat in the butter. Chill 3 hours. Form teaspoons of the mixture into balls. Chill again, then roll in the ground almonds. Place a whole almond in each ball.

Makes about 60.

CHEESE PUFF BALLS

½ cup grated Parmesan cheese
1 tablespoon flour
¼ teaspoon salt
Dash of cayenne pepper

2 egg whites, stiffly beaten
3 tablespoons cracker crumbs
Fat for deep frying

Mix the cheese, flour, salt and pepper; fold into the egg whites; if too dry to mold, add a few drops of milk. Shape in small balls, roll in crumbs and fry in deep 375° fat 1 minute or until golden brown; drain on absorbent paper.

Makes about 18.

CROÛTES AU FROMAGE (Cheese Crusts)

1¼ cups sifted flour
⅛ teaspoon salt
Dash cayenne pepper
¼ pound (1 stick) butter
1 cup grated cheddar cheese

3 tablespoons heavy cream
1 egg, beaten
1 cup grated Gruyère or Swiss cheese

Sift the flour, salt and cayenne into a bowl; cut in 6 tablespoons of the butter and the cheddar cheese. Stir in the cream until a ball of dough is formed. Chill 2 hours.

Roll out the dough ⅛ inch thick. Cut into circles with a 2-inch cooky cutter. Brush with egg and arrange on a cooky sheet. Bake 7 minutes or until delicately browned.

Cream the remaining butter with the Gruyère cheese. While the pastry is hot, spread the mixture on half the rounds and make sandwiches. Return to oven to heat.

Makes about 20 sandwiches.

FROMAGE À LA GELÉE (Jellied Cheese, French Style)

1 teaspoon gelatin	2 tablespoons grated cheddar
½ cup dry white wine	cheese
½ cup heavy cream	½ teaspoon prepared mustard
¼ teaspoon salt	Dash cayenne pepper
2 tablespoons grated Parmesan cheese	

Soften the gelatin in the wine, then place over hot water, stirring until dissolved. Chill until gelatin begins to set. Whip the cream with the salt. Beat the gelatin with an electric or rotary beater, then gradually beat in the whipped cream.

Mix the cheeses with mustard and cayenne pepper. Add to the gelatin mixture, beating until well blended. Turn into paper petit-four cups and chill until firm. Remove from the cups and serve with crisp crackers.

Makes about 12.

Note: If you prefer, drop the mixture onto a lightly oiled pan by the teaspoon and shape into mounds. Serve on crackers.

SPIEDINI ALLA ROMANA (Cheese and Anchovy Appetizer, Roman Style)

4 slices white bread	1 clove garlic, minced
1 pound mozzarella cheese	3 tablespoons wine vinegar
½ cup melted butter	¼ teaspoon freshly ground black
3 tablespoons olive oil	pepper
½ cup chopped anchovies	2 tablespoons minced parsley

Trim the crusts and cut the bread into ¾-inch squares. Cut the cheese the same size. Thread the bread and cheese on 16 small skewers or toothpicks, starting and ending with the bread. (Use about 5 pieces of bread and 4 of cheese for each skewer.) Arrange the skewers on a buttered baking pan; brush all sides with melted butter. Bake in a preheated 400° oven 5 minutes. Prepare the sauce while the skewers are baking.

Heat the oil; stir in the anchovies and garlic until anchovies dissolve. Add the vinegar, pepper and parsley; pour over the skewered ingredients and bake 5 minutes longer, turning the skewers to brown all sides. Serve hot.

Makes 16.

CHEESE ROLL

½ pound Roquefort or blue cheese
½ pound cream cheese
4 tablespoons butter
3 tablespoons cognac

2 tablespoons grated onions
½ cup chopped stuffed olives
¾ cup ground toasted almonds

Have the Roquefort, cream cheese and butter at room temperature and beat together until smooth. Mix in the cognac, onions and olives. Shape into rolls 1½ inches in diameter and 4 inches long. Coat with the almonds. Chill.

With a very sharp knife, cut into ¼-inch slices and serve on toast rounds or crackers.

Makes about 24.

CHEESE MOLD

Thinly sliced white bread
Thinly sliced pumpernickel
¾ pound butter

¼ pound Roquefort cheese
½ pound Camembert cheese
¼ cup whipped cream

Butter a 9-inch loaf pan. Cut the white bread and pumpernickel in the same shapes and line the pan with them, alternating the breads.

Cream the butter until very fluffy, then beat in the cheeses until very smooth. Fold in the whipped cream. Spread over the bread. Chill 4 hours or overnight. Carefully turn out and cut in narrow strips.

FRIED CHEESE LOGS

¼ pound Camembert cheese, rind removed
1 3-ounce package cream cheese
3 tablespoons butter
3 tablespoons cornstarch
¾ cup milk

½ teaspoon salt
Dash cayenne pepper
¼ cup sifted flour
2 egg yolks, beaten
¾ cup dry bread crumbs
Vegetable oil for deep frying

In a saucepan, mash the Camembert and cream cheese until smooth. Cream the butter and add to the cheese with the cornstarch, mixing well. Stir in the milk, salt and cayenne pepper. Cook over low heat until thick and smooth, about 5 minutes.

Pour onto a plate to cool. Form into logs ½ inch round and 1 inch long. Roll them in flour, then egg yolks, and then bread crumbs, coating them well.

Heat the oil to 380° and drop the logs into it. Fry until lightly browned. Drain.

Makes about 12.

CHEESE SNAPS

2 cups (½ pound) grated Swiss cheese
1 egg yolk
¼ teaspoon salt
¼ teaspoon freshly ground black pepper

1 egg white, stiffly beaten
12 thin slices white bread, trimmed
Vegetable oil for deep frying

Blend cheese, egg yolk, salt and pepper until smooth. Fold in the egg white thoroughly.

Spread the cheese mixture on 6 slices of the bread. Cover with remaining slices, pressing down well. Cut in half. Set aside for 10 minutes.

Heat the oil to 375°; carefully place the sandwiches in it. Fry until lightly browned. Drain. Makes 12.

SABLÉS SUISSE (Swiss Cheese Biscuits)

1¼ cups sifted flour
½ teaspoon salt
⅛ teaspoon pepper
⅛ teaspoon nutmeg
Dash cayenne pepper

¼ pound (1 stick) butter
1 cup (¼ pound) grated Swiss cheese
2 eggs, beaten

Sift together the flour, salt, pepper, nutmeg and cayenne pepper. Cut in the butter with a pastry blender or two knives. Add the cheese and eggs, mixing until a dough is formed (if not proper consistency to roll, add a little water). Chill for 2 hours.

143

Roll out ¼ inch thick on a lightly floured board. Cut into desired shapes. Arrange on a buttered cooky sheet. Bake in a preheated 375° oven 10 minutes, or until delicately browned.

Makes about 32 2-inch biscuits.

GALETTES AU FROMAGE (Rich French Cheese Wafers)

½ pound (2 cups) grated Swiss cheese	¾ teaspoon salt
½ cup grated Parmesan cheese	⅛ teaspoon cayenne pepper
½ pound (2 sticks) butter, at room temperature	⅛ teaspoon nutmeg
¾ cup sifted flour	1 egg
	1 teaspoon water

Knead together 1½ cups of the Swiss cheese, the Parmesan cheese, butter, flour, salt, cayenne pepper and nutmeg. Form into a ball and chill 15 minutes. Break off tablespoons of the mixture, form into balls, then flatten into circles about ¼ inch thick. Arrange on a baking sheet, leaving space between each. Brush with the egg beaten with the water, then sprinkle with a little of the remaining Swiss cheese. Bake in a preheated 425° oven 10 minutes or until puffed and browned. Cool on a cake rack. Makes about 40.

STUFFED EDAM CHEESE

1 whole Edam cheese	1 teaspoon Worcestershire sauce
½ cup dry sherry	Dash cayenne pepper
1½ teaspoons prepared mustard	

Remove the red waxed coating of the cheese. Cut a 2-inch piece off the top. Carefully scoop out the cheese, leaving a 1-inch-thick shell. Grate the scooped-out cheese and blend with the sherry, mustard, Worcestershire sauce and cayenne pepper. Stuff the shell. Serve with crisp crackers or thinly sliced pumpernickel.

SWISS CHEESE CUBES IN KIRSCH

1 slice Swiss cheese, cut ½ inch thick.
¾ cup kirsch (cherry liqueur)

Trim the rind off the cheese, then cut in ½-inch cubes. Marinate in the kirsch in the refrigerator, covered, for 3 hours. Pierce with cocktail picks and arrange in a small serving bowl, with the kirsch on the bottom.
Makes 64.

CHEESE OLIVES

4 tablespoons cream cheese	18 large pimiento-stuffed green
4 tablespoons grated cheddar cheese	olives
3 tablespoons heavy cream	1 cup chopped almonds
½ teaspoon Worcestershire sauce	

Beat together the cream cheese, cheddar cheese, cream and Worcestershire sauce until smooth. Roll the olives in the mixture until well coated, then in the almonds. Chill.
Makes 18.

FISH AND SHELLFISH

MOST AMERICANS think of fish as something they eat on Friday, but with comparatively little relish. In our country, unfortunately, fish is seldom prepared with imagination. Regretfully, we must admit that the Europeans do better with fish dishes than we do. In France, for example, most dinners of an elaborate nature always have a fish course, usually very well prepared.

By and large, Americans are meat eaters. Nineteen times out of twenty, guests at a dinner party will be offered meat as a main course. An enterprising hostess, although aware of the national preference for meat, can capitalize upon this by serving a fish hors d'oeuvre. It offers an interesting contrast with the meat that will subsequently follow in the meal, and if several hors d'oeuvres are served, certainly at least one of them should be prepared with fish.

The national palate, however, does approve strongly of shellfish, and American shellfish are truly excellent. Shrimp, in particular, is outstandingly popular. A standard hors d'oeuvre is cold boiled shrimp with a bowl of cocktail sauce for dunking. This is a good appetizer, but certainly not one that is novel or imaginative, and the shrimp hors d'oeuvres in this section are far more interesting.

Chinese shrimp balls are highly regarded by gourmets as an outstanding contribution to the world of fine food. A German-Jewish preparation, Gefüllter Fisch, fish balls, is exceptionally good, having both an excellent taste and a fine texture. A white dill sauce is used in Austria to accentuate the natural qualities of shrimp. An Italian dish of shrimp broiled in a lemon-garlic sauce is extremely popular in the United States; although called scampi, scampi are actually a type of shellfish resembling shrimp but found only in the Adriatic Sea. England, rarely in the forefront of culinary endeavors, features an interesting manner of preparing shrimp, English potted shrimp.

FLUFFY FISH BALLS

2 pounds sole, pike, salmon	½ teaspoon pepper
¼ pound softened butter	¼ cup heavy cream
¼ cup flour	½ cup vegetable oil
2 teaspoons salt	

Remove the skin and bones of the fish. Grind or chop the fish very fine. Cream the butter, flour, salt and pepper, and work mixture into the fish. Beat until very smooth then mix in the cream. Shape into 1-inch balls.

Heat the oil in a skillet and fry the balls until browned on all sides. Serve with tartar sauce.

Makes about 36.

FLUFFY FISH BALLS, CHINESE STYLE

1 pound white-meat fish fillets	½ teaspoon ground ginger
2 cups water	¼ teaspoon monosodium glutamate
2 egg whites	Vegetable oil for deep frying
3 tablespoons cornstarch	2 tablespoons soy sauce
2 teaspoons dry sherry	1 tablespoon vinegar
1 teaspoon salt	1 tablespoon sugar

Put the fish through the fine blade of a food chopper, gradually adding 1 cup water while grinding. Or blend in an electric blender. Beat the egg whites until stiff, gradually adding 2 tablespoons of the cornstarch. Combine with ground fish, the sherry, salt, ginger and monosodium glutamate. Mix thoroughly.

Form teaspoons of the mixture into balls. Heat the oil to 370°. Fry the balls until browned. Drain. Mix the remaining cornstarch with remaining water. Heat the soy sauce, vinegar and sugar and stir in the cornstarch mixture until thickened. Serve fish balls hot, with the sauce in separate bowl.

Makes about 36.

FRIED CHINESE SHRIMP BALLS

2 pounds raw shrimp, shelled and deveined	¾ teaspoon salt
	¼ teaspoon white pepper
6 water chestnuts	2 tablespoons ice water
⅛ pound pork fat	¾ cup cornstarch
3 green onions	Vegetable oil for deep frying
3 egg whites	

Wash and drain the shrimp. Grind or chop until very fine with the water chestnuts, pork fat and green onions. With the hands, mix in the egg whites, salt, pepper, water and ¼ cup of the cornstarch. Pick up the mixture and bang it down on a firm surface several times, or until mixture sticks together. Form teaspoons of the mixture into balls and roll them in the cornstarch.

Heat the oil to 365° and fry the balls until golden brown. Drain. Serve as soon as possible, as the balls tend to shrink when they cool. Makes about 36.

GEFÜLLTER FISCH (Fish Balls, German-Jewish Style)

2 pounds fillets of fresh-water fish (carp, pike, whitefish)	2 tablespoons cracker or matzo meal
3 large onions	1 egg, beaten
½ teaspoon sugar	¼ cup cold water
2 teaspoons salt	2 carrots, sliced
1 teaspoon freshly ground white pepper	4 cups boiling water
	Head, skin and bones of fish

147

Grind the fish fillets and 1 onion in a meat chopper. Mix the ground fish and onion, sugar, 1 teaspoon salt, ½ teaspoon pepper, cracker meal, egg and cold water in a wooden bowl and chop until fine and well blended. Or put all the above ingredients in an electric blender and blend until smooth.

Slice the remaining onions. Put in a pan with the carrots, boiling water, fish head, skin and bones and remaining salt and pepper. Bring to a boil and cook 20 minutes. Shape the ground-fish mixture into walnut-sized balls between wet palms and drop into pan. Cover loosely and cook over low heat 1 hour, shaking the pan occasionally. Taste for seasoning. Remove fish balls with a slotted spoon. Chill and serve very cold, pierced with cocktail or toothpicks and with horseradish as a dip.

Makes about 60.

CRAB-MEAT BALLS

1 pound crab meat
3 tablespoons minced onions
1½ teaspoons salt
¼ teaspoon white pepper
½ teaspoon dry mustard
2 egg yolks

2 tablespoons dry sherry
2 tablespoons minced parsley
¼ cup dry bread crumbs
¾ cup ground almonds
Vegetable oil for deep frying

Flake the crab meat and combine with the onions, salt, pepper, mustard, egg yolks, sherry and parsley. Shape into walnut-sized balls; roll in a mixture of the bread crumbs and almonds. Heat the oil to 375° and fry the balls until delicately browned. Drain well and pierce with cocktail picks.

Makes about 50.

CURRIED CRAB-MEAT BALLS, INDIAN STYLE

¾ cup minced onions
4 tablespoons butter
½ cup fine grated coconut
1 pound crab meat
1¼ teaspoons salt
2 teaspoons curry powder

1 clove garlic, minced
1 egg
2 tablespoons cold water
½ cup dry bread crumbs
½ cup vegetable oil

Sauté the onions in 2 tablespoons butter until lightly browned. Remove onions. Sauté the coconut in the remaining butter until lightly browned. Combine the onions, coconut, crab meat, salt, curry powder, garlic, egg and water in a blender container. Blend until very smooth (or chop ingredients until smooth). Form into walnut-sized balls and roll in the bread crumbs.

Heat the oil in a skillet; brown the balls on all sides. Drain and pierce with cocktail picks. Makes about 50.

GROUND PORK AND CRAB-MEAT BALLS, CHINESE STYLE

1½ pounds ground pork
¼ pound crab meat
1½ teaspoons salt
½ teaspoon freshly ground black pepper
1 teaspoon sugar

½ cup chopped mushrooms
½ cup chopped water chestnuts
¾ cup cornstarch
2 eggs
2 tablespoons water
Vegetable oil for deep frying

Chop together the pork, crab meat, salt, pepper, sugar, mushrooms and water chestnuts until very fine. Shape into walnut-sized balls. Roll in the cornstarch, then in the eggs beaten with the water.

Heat the oil to 360°. Fry the balls until browned on all sides, about 10 minutes. Drain and pierce with cocktail picks. Makes about 60.

BALTIMORE CRAB CAKES

1½ pounds lump crab meat
6 tablespoons butter
¼ cup minced celery
½ cup minced green pepper
¼ cup grated onions
1 tablespoon lemon juice
6 tablespoons flour

2 cups milk
1 teaspoon salt
½ teaspoon A.1. Sauce
2 drops Tabasco
2 eggs, beaten
1 cup dry bread crumbs
Vegetable oil for deep frying

Pick over the crab meat, removing any cartilage, but leave the crab meat in large pieces. Melt 2 tablespoons butter in a

149

skillet; sauté the celery and green pepper 10 minutes, then mix in the onions and lemon juice. Remove from heat.

Melt the remaining butter in a saucepan; blend in the flour, then the milk, stirring steadily to the boiling point. Cook over low heat 5 minutes; stir in the salt, A.1. Sauce and Tabasco. Beat the eggs in a bowl; gradually add the hot sauce, stirring steadily to prevent curdling. Cool 10 minutes; stir in the crab meat and sautéed vegetables. Form into walnut-sized balls, flatten slightly and roll in the bread crumbs. Heat the oil to 375° and fry the cakes in it until browned. Drain and pierce with cocktail picks.

Makes about 60.

CAROLINA BAKED CRAB MEAT

1 pound crab meat	½ cup dry white wine
3 tablespoons butter	½ teaspoon salt
3 tablespoons flour	½ teaspoon pepper
¾ cup light cream	2 tablespoons minced pimientos
½ cup bottled clam juice	8 slices toast, cut in thirds
¾ cup grated Parmesan cheese	

Pick over the crab meat, removing any cartilage.

Melt the butter in a saucepan. Blend in the flour. Gradually add the cream and clam juice, stirring constantly until the boiling point. Cook over low heat 5 minutes. Add the crab meat, ½ cup cheese, the wine, salt, pepper and pimientos, mixing lightly. Cook 5 minutes.

Spread the crab meat on the toast and sprinkle with remaining cheese. Place under the broiler until browned.

Makes 24.

SHRIMP IN DILL SAUCE, AUSTRIAN STYLE

4 tablespoons butter	¼ teaspoon freshly ground black pepper
½ cup minced onions	
2 pounds raw shrimp, shelled and deveined	2 cups sour cream
2 tablespoons flour	¼ cup minced dill or 1 tablespoon dill seed
1½ teaspoons salt	

Melt the butter in a deep skillet; sauté the onions 5 minutes. Mix in the shrimp; sauté 4 minutes. Sprinkle with the flour, salt and pepper; cook 1 minute. Stir in the sour cream and dill; heat but do not let boil. Serve shrimp and sauce in a chafing dish or over a candle warmer to keep hot, and surround with cocktail picks for spearing.

Makes about 36.

SHRIMP IN MUSTARD SAUCE, GERMAN STYLE

2 green onions, chopped fine	2 teaspoons paprika
2 hard-cooked eggs, mashed	Dash cayenne pepper
1 cup olive oil	2 pounds shrimp, cooked, shelled
1/3 cup wine vinegar	and deveined
1/2 teaspoon salt	
4 tablespoons prepared mustard	

Combine all the ingredients but the shrimp in a blender bowl and blend until smooth, or chop the onions and eggs to a paste, then gradually beat in the remaining ingredients. Pour over the shrimp, and turn shrimp several times to coat with the sauce. Chill 3 hours before serving. Pierce with cocktail picks.

Makes about 36.

CHEESE-STUFFED SHRIMP

2 pounds jumbo shrimp, cooked	2 teaspoons minced green onions
1 3-ounce package cream cheese	1/2 teaspoon prepared mustard
3 tablespoons Roquefort or blue cheese	3/4 cup minced parsley

Remove the shells of the shrimp, and with a sharp knife split the shrimp down the spine halfway through, discarding the vein.

Mash the cream cheese and Roquefort smooth; blend in the green onions and mustard. Stuff the shrimp with the mixture, pressing the cut sides together gently, then dip the cheese side in the parsley. Pierce with cocktail picks. Chill.

Makes about 30.

GLAZED SHRIMP

½ cup olive oil
3 tablespoons wine vinegar
¼ teaspoon salt
⅛ teaspoon freshly ground black pepper

¼ cup chili sauce
1 envelope (tablespoon) gelatin
¼ cup dry white wine
2 pounds shrimp, cooked, shelled and deveined

Shake or beat together the oil, vinegar, salt, pepper and chili sauce.

Stir the gelatin into the wine; place over hot water, stirring until dissolved. Mix into dressing and chill until just beginning to set. Pierce each shrimp with a cocktail pick or toothpick. Dip the shrimp into the gelatin mixture. Chill until partially set, then dip into the gelatin mixture again. Chill again until firmly set.

Makes about 36.

SHRIMP IN CHINESE TOMATO SAUCE

1½ pounds raw shrimp, shelled and deveined
½ cup cornstarch
2 eggs, beaten
1 cup dry bread crumbs
1 quart vegetable oil
¾ cup sliced green onions
¼ cup diced water chestnuts

1 clove minced garlic
1 teaspoon minced preserved ginger
1 cup water
¼ cup ketchup
2 tablespoons sugar
2 teaspoons soy sauce
1 teaspoon vinegar

Wash and dry the shrimp. Toss the shrimp with the cornstarch (reserve 1 tablespoon), dip in the eggs, then roll in the bread crumbs.

Heat the oil (reserve 3 tablespoons) to 365°. Fry the shrimp in it until golden brown. Drain, place on a serving dish and keep warm.

Heat the 3 tablespoons oil in a skillet; sauté the green onions, water chestnuts, garlic and ginger 3 minutes. Mix the reserved cornstarch with the water. Add the ketchup, sugar, soy sauce and vinegar. Stir the cornstarch into the skillet until thickened. Pour over the shrimp and serve hot, surrounded with picks.

Makes about 24.

SHRIMP IN YOGURT, PAKISTANI STYLE

2 pounds raw shrimp, shelled and
  deveined
3 tablespoons butter
½ cup chopped onions
1 teaspoon salt

½ teaspoon turmeric
½ teaspoon powdered coriander
¼ cup yogurt
Dash cayenne pepper

Wash and dry the shrimp. Melt the butter in a skillet; sauté the onions 5 minutes. Add the shrimp, salt, turmeric and coriander. Cook over medium heat 5 minutes, turning the shrimp once to brown both sides. Mix in the yogurt and cayenne pepper. Bring to a boil and cook over medium heat 5 minutes, stirring a few times. Pierce with cocktail picks.

Makes about 36.

BROILED SHRIMP IN LEMON-GARLIC BUTTER, ITALIAN STYLE

2 pounds raw shrimp
½ cup (1 stick) butter
2 cloves garlic, minced
3 tablespoons lemon juice

1¼ teaspoons salt
¼ teaspoon white pepper
3 tablespoons minced parsley

Remove the shells from the shrimp, but leave the tail part. Cut down the back, remove black vein, rinse and dry. Melt the butter in a skillet; add the garlic, lemon juice, salt and pepper. Cook over low heat 1 minute, but do not let brown. Place the shrimp in a buttered shallow baking pan. Pour the butter mixture over the shrimp. Broil 4 inches under the heat 7 minutes, turning the shrimp after 3 minutes. Sprinkle with the parsley. Pierce with cocktail picks and serve hot.

Makes about 36.

CEYLON SPICED BROILED SHRIMP

2 pounds raw shrimp, shelled and
  deveined
1 cup vegetable oil
1 teaspoon salt
¼ teaspoon freshly ground black
  pepper

1 teaspoon chili powder
2 teaspoons turmeric
1 teaspoon basil
¼ teaspoon mint
2 cloves garlic, minced

Wash and dry the shrimp. Marinate in a mixture of the remaining ingredients in the refrigerator for at least 12 hours.

Drain the shrimp and arrange in a broiling pan. Broil as close to the heat as possible, basting a few times with some of the marinade, 4 minutes on each side. Pierce with cocktail picks and serve hot.

Makes about 36.

SHRIMP DIABLE, ITALIAN STYLE

1 cup vegetable oil	1 clove garlic, minced
2 tablespoons prepared mustard	2 tablespoons minced onions
2 teaspoons prepared horseradish	½ cup wine vinegar
2 tablespoons chili sauce	½ cup dry white wine
1 teaspoon salt	2 pounds shrimp, cooked, shelled
⅛ teaspoon Tabasco	and deveined
1 teaspoon paprika	

Mix together all the ingredients but the shrimp. Pour over the shrimp; let marinate in the refrigerator overnight or for at least 4 hours. Drain and pierce with cocktail picks.

Makes about 36.

DEVILED SHRIMP CREOLE

2 pounds raw shrimp, shelled and deveined	1½ teaspoons salt
	¼ teaspoon thyme
1 cup dry white wine	1 bay leaf
¼ cup cognac	2 tablespoons heavy cream
3 sprigs parsley	2 tablespoons dry sherry
1 carrot, sliced	1 cup mayonnaise
1 onion	¼ cup chopped pimiento-stuffed
1 clove garlic, split	olives

Wash and drain the shrimp. Combine the wine, cognac, parsley, carrot, onion, garlic, salt, thyme and bay leaf in a saucepan. Bring to a boil, add the shrimp and cook over low heat 8 minutes. Let cool in the liquid. Drain thoroughly.

Blend the cream and sherry with the mayonnaise; fold in the olives. Heap in a bowl and hang the shrimp on the edges.

Makes about 36.

SPICED SHRIMP

2 cups water
2 cups dry white wine
2 teaspoons salt
¼ teaspoon Tabasco
2 cloves
3 allspice
6 peppercorns

2 bay leaves
2 cloves garlic, minced
1 cup chopped celery and leaves
6 sprigs parsley
2 pounds raw shrimp, shelled and
   deveined

Combine and bring to a boil all the ingredients but the shrimp. Add the shrimp, bring to a boil again and cook over low heat 6 minutes. Cool the shrimp in the liquid, then chill at least 4 hours. Drain thoroughly. Pierce with cocktail picks.

Makes about 36.

SHRIMP IN PAPERS

¼ pound Roquefort cheese
½ pound cream cheese
¾ cup dry white wine
½ cup chopped stuffed green olives

1½ pounds raw shrimp, shelled,
   deveined and halved
6 slices lemon, cut in thirds

Cream the Roquefort cheese and cream cheese until smooth; add the wine then gradually the olives.

Cut 18 pieces of parchment paper or aluminum foil about 4 inches square; divide the cheese mixture among them and cover with several pieces of shrimp and a lemon piece. Bring two edges of the paper together and make two folds. Bring up other sides, and twist to make a secure closing. Bake in a 400° oven 20 minutes. Serve in the papers. Makes 18.

ESCABECHE DE CAMARONES (Pickled Shrimp, Mexican Style)

4 large onions
¾ cup olive oil
3 cloves garlic, chopped
2 pounds raw shrimp, shelled and
   deveined
½ cup wine vinegar
1½ teaspoons salt

½ teaspoon freshly ground black
   pepper
¼ teaspoon dry mustard
¼ teaspoon dried ground chili
   peppers or 2 pickled chili peppers
   (jalapeños), cut into strips

Chop two of the onions and slice the remaining two. Heat ¼ cup of the oil in a skillet; sauté the chopped onions and the garlic 10 minutes. Add the shrimp and sauté 7 minutes. Remove from heat and cool 15 minutes. Mix the sliced onions, remaining oil, vinegar, salt, pepper, mustard and chili peppers in a bowl. Add the shrimp and baste. Marinate in the refrigerator 24-48 hours, basting several times. Drain and pierce with cocktail picks. Makes about 36.

MARINATED SHRIMP, CALIFORNIA STYLE

1 cup chopped green onions	1 teaspoon salt
1 clove garlic, minced	⅛ teaspoon Tabasco
¼ cup chopped parsley	2 tablespoons drained capers
½ cup olive oil	2 pounds shrimp, cooked, shelled
½ cup dry vermouth	and deveined
2 tablespoons wine vinegar	3 avocados

Chop to a paste the onions, garlic and parsley. Mix in the oil, vermouth, vinegar, salt, Tabasco and capers. Pour over the shrimp and let marinate overnight in the refrigerator, basting and turning frequently. Drain, reserving the marinade.

Peel the avocados and cut in cubes, the same number as the shrimp. Toss in the marinade and drain. Put one cube of avocado and one shrimp on each cocktail pick.

Makes about 36.

PACIFIC ISLANDS SHRIMP

1½ pounds small raw shrimp,	1 teaspoon salt
shelled and deveined	½ teaspoon freshly ground black
1 cup lime or lemon juice	pepper
½ cup finely chopped onions	

Split the shrimp in half lengthwise; wash and dry. Combine in a bowl (not metal) with the lime juice and onions. Marinate for at least 4 hours in the refrigerator. Season with the salt and pepper before serving. Surround with picks.

Makes about 28.

Note: Don't worry about the shrimp being raw. The citrus juice gives them a cooked flavor.

ENGLISH POTTED SHRIMP

1 pound shrimp, cooked, shelled and deveined
¼ pound (1 stick) butter

Dash cayenne pepper
¼ teaspoon nutmeg
Salt

Chop the shrimp coarsely (unless you're able to obtain very tiny shrimp, or use the canned Danish variety). Melt the butter in a skillet; add the shrimp. Cook over very low heat 3 minutes, stirring frequently. Season with the cayenne pepper, nutmeg and salt to taste. Pack into a bowl or crock, being sure to add all the melted butter. Chill until butter solidifies.

Makes about 2 cups.

COCONUT FRIED SHRIMP, POLYNESIAN STYLE

2 pounds raw shrimp
¼ cup lemon juice
½ teaspoon salt
¼ teaspoon ground ginger
2 teaspoons curry powder

1¾ cups flour
2 teaspoons baking powder
1¾ cups milk
1½ cups fine grated coconut
Vegetable oil for deep frying

Shell and devein the shrimp, cutting about halfway through. Wash and dry, then marinate in a mixture of the lemon juice, salt, ginger and curry powder 2 hours in the refrigerator, turning the shrimp occasionally. Drain, reserving the marinade.

Make a batter of 1⅓ cups of the flour, the baking powder, milk and marinade. Toss the shrimp in the remaining flour, dip in the batter, coating them heavily, then roll in the coconut.

Heat the oil to 375° and fry the shrimp in it, a few at a time, until browned, about 4 minutes. Drain. Keep in a 350° oven while preparing the balance. Serve with chopped chutney as a dip.

Makes about 36.

KAUAI (Hawaiian Broiled Shrimp in Pineapple Sauce)

1½ tablespoons cornstarch
1 cup pineapple juice
3 tablespoons honey
½ cup soy sauce

2 tablespoons vinegar
1 teaspoon powdered ginger
36 shrimp, cooked and cleaned

Mix the cornstarch with a little pineapple juice, then combine with all the pineapple juice, the honey, soy sauce, vinegar and ginger. Cook over low heat, stirring constantly until thickened.

Using 18 skewers, thread 2 shrimp on each, and dip in the sauce. Broil until delicately browned on all sides. Baste occasionally.

Makes 36.

SHRIMP REMOULADE, NEW ORLEANS STYLE

¼ cup olive oil
4 tablespoons lemon juice
¼ cup prepared Creole mustard
3 tablespoons prepared horseradish
1 clove garlic, minced
⅛ teaspoon Tabasco

¼ cup minced shallots or green
   onions
¼ cup minced parsley
2 pounds shrimp, cooked, shelled
   and deveined

Beat together the oil, lemon juice, mustard, horseradish, garlic and Tabasco. Mix in the shallots and parsley. Pour over the shrimp and marinate in the refrigerator at least 3 hours before serving. Drain and pierce with cocktail picks.

Makes about 36.

FRIED SHRIMP IN EGG BATTER

2 pounds raw shrimp
3 eggs
1 cup milk
1 cup sifted flour

1 teaspoon salt
4 tablespoons cornstarch
1 quart vegetable oil

Remove the shells and veins, but leave the tails on the shrimp. Cut the shrimp down the back. Wash and dry; open the shrimp and flatten with a cleaver or heavy knife. Beat together the eggs, milk, flour, salt and cornstarch until a smooth batter is formed. Heat the oil to 375°. Hold each shrimp by the tail and dip it into the batter, coating it well. Fry until browned. Drain and serve with warm chili sauce as a dip.

Makes about 36.

SCAMPI FRITTI (Fried Shrimp, Italian Style)

1½ pounds raw shrimp, shelled and deveined
1/3 cup flour
1½ teaspoons salt

½ teaspoon freshly ground black pepper
1 cup olive or vegetable oil
Lemon wedges

Wash and dry the shrimp; toss in a mixture of the flour, salt and pepper. Heat the oil in a skillet; fry the shrimp until browned on both sides. Drain. Serve with the lemon wedges.

Makes about 24.

PHILIPPINE STUFFED SHRIMP

1½ pounds large raw shrimp
¼ pound ground beef
3 tablespoons chopped water chestnuts
3 tablespoons chopped green onions

2 teaspoons salt
⅛ teaspoon Tabasco
½ cup cornstarch
Vegetable oil for deep frying

Shell the shrimp, leaving the tails intact. Slit the backs fairly deep and discard the black veins. Wash and dry.

Mix together the beef, water chestnuts, green onions, 1 teaspoon salt and the Tabasco. Stuff the shrimp with the mixture, press gently together, and if necessary, fasten with wooden toothpicks. Roll the shrimp in a mixture of the cornstarch and remaining salt.

Heat the oil to 370° and fry the shrimp in it until browned, about 5 minutes. Drain, discard the toothpicks and pierce with cocktail picks. Serve hot.

Makes about 20.

STUFFED FRIED SHRIMP

½ cup minced lobster	1½ teaspoons salt
¼ pound red snapper or white-meat fish	⅛ teaspoon pepper
	Dash cayenne pepper
42 large raw shrimp, shelled and deveined	⅛ teaspoon celery salt
	⅛ teaspoon nutmeg
¼ cup minced onions	¾ cup light cream
¼ teaspoon minced garlic	2 egg yolks, beaten
6 tablespoons butter	Vegetable oil for deep frying
½ cup flour	

Finely chop the lobster, the snapper and 8 of the shrimp; sauté with the onions and garlic in 3 tablespoons of the butter for 10 minutes, stirring frequently.

Melt the remaining butter in a saucepan; stir in 2 tablespoons flour, the salt, pepper, cayenne, celery salt and nutmeg. Gradually add the cream, stirring steadily to the boiling point. Cook over low heat 5 minutes. Add to the egg yolks gradually, stirring steadily to prevent curdling. Blend in the fish mixture and chill.

Split the remaining shrimp and stuff with the previous mixture. Press together firmly. Roll in the remaining flour. Heat the fat to 370° and fry the shrimp in it until browned. Drain and serve at once.

Makes 34.

ROQUEFORT-STUFFED SHRIMP

1½ teaspoons salt	¼ pound Roquefort cheese
1 stalk celery	¼ pound cream cheese
½ teaspoon pickling spice	1½ tablespoons mayonnaise
3 cups water	¾ cup finely chopped parsley
2 pounds large raw shrimp	

Buy very large shrimp—about 15 to the pound. In a saucepan, combine the salt, celery, pickling spice and water. Bring to a boil and add the shrimp. Cook over low heat 6 minutes. Drain and cool. Shell the shrimp and carefully remove the black vein. Split halfway through the deveined side and force open slightly.

Cream together the Roquefort, cream cheese and mayonnaise. Stuff the shrimp and roll in the parsley. Arrange on a serving dish. The shrimp may be served as an hors d'oeuvre, pierced with cocktail picks, or as an appetizer on individual plates.

Makes about 30.

INDIAN SHRIMP CROQUETTES

2 pounds raw shrimp, shelled and
   deveined
1 tablespoon chopped dill
1 tablespoon chopped parsley
1 teaspoon salt

½ teaspoon ground cumin
2 teaspoons grated lemon rind
1 egg, beaten
¾ cup ground almonds
6 tablespoons butter

Wash and drain the shrimp. Purée a few shrimp at a time in an electric blender or chop to a paste. Mix in the dill, parsley, salt, cumin, lemon rind and egg until well blended. Shape by the tablespoon into small croquettes and dip in the almonds.

Melt the butter in a skillet; sauté the croquettes over low heat until browned on both sides and cooked through, about 5 minutes. Serve hot.

Makes about 30.

SHRIMP CROQUETTES

1 pound raw shrimp, shelled and
   deveined
2 tablespoons butter
¾ cup finely chopped onions
1 clove garlic, minced
1 slice white bread
¼ cup milk

1 tablespoon minced parsley
1½ teaspoons salt
¼ teaspoon freshly ground black
   pepper
2 eggs
½ cup dry bread crumbs
¼ cup salad oil

Chop the shrimp very fine. Melt the butter in a skillet; sauté the onions and garlic until golden brown. Soak the bread in the milk; drain and mash smooth. Mix together the shrimp, bread, sautéed onions, parsley, salt, pepper and 1 egg. Form heaping teaspoons of the mixture into croquettes. Beat remaining egg, dip croquettes in it, then in bread crumbs.

Heat the oil in a skillet and fry the croquettes until browned on both sides. Serve hot.

Makes about 24.

SHRIMP CURLS

1½ pounds raw shrimp, shelled and deveined
¾ teaspoon salt
½ teaspoon freshly ground black pepper
½ teaspoon powdered ginger
3 tablespoons vegetable oil

¼ cup sliced green onions
1 teaspoon cornstarch
¼ cup chili sauce
2 tablespoons soy sauce
2 tablespoons cider vinegar
1 clove garlic, minced

Wash and dry the shrimp, toss with the salt, pepper and ginger. Heat the oil in a skillet; sauté the shrimp and green onions 2 minutes, stirring frequently. Mix together the cornstarch, chili sauce, soy sauce, vinegar and garlic. Add to the shrimp; bring to a boil and cook over low heat 5 minutes. Heap in a hot bowl, with some picks on the side for spearing, and serve hot. Makes about 28.

SHRIMP TOAST, CHINESE STYLE

1 pound raw shrimp, shelled and deveined
1 teaspoon minced ginger
1 teaspoon dry sherry
1 teaspoon salt
1 egg white

1 teaspoon cornstarch
Dash monosodium glutamate
8 slices bread, trimmed
2 tablespoons chopped ham
2 tablespoons chopped parsley
Vegetable oil for deep frying

Chop the shrimp very fine. Mix in the ginger, sherry, salt, unbeaten egg white, cornstarch and monosodium glutamate. Mix thoroughly. Cut each slice of bread into 4 squares and spread some shrimp mixture on each. Sprinkle shrimp with ham and parsley and press down lightly. Heat the oil to 370° and fry the squares first with shrimp-mixture side down, then turn over and fry until bread is golden brown. Drain. Serve hot.

Makes 32.

SHRIMP CAKES

2 egg yolks
½ cup heavy cream
½ teaspoon salt
Dash cayenne pepper
¾ cup sifted flour
2 tablespoons grated onions

1 tablespoon melted butter
¼ cup grated Parmesan cheese
1 cup chopped cooked shrimp
2 egg whites
1 cup vegetable oil

Beat together the egg yolks, cream, salt and cayenne pepper. Beat in the flour until smooth, then mix in the onions, melted butter and cheese. Chill 1 hour, then fold in the shrimp. Beat the egg whites until stiff but not dry; fold into the shrimp mixture.

Heat the oil in a skillet until it bubbles; drop the mixture into it by the scant tablespoon. Fry until browned on both sides. As the pancakes are browned, drain and keep hot while preparing the balance. Makes about 24.

FISH-SHRIMP CAKES, AFRICAN STYLE

¾ pound fish fillets
¾ pound raw shrimp, shelled and deveined
3 slices bacon
1 cup ground peanuts

2 tablespoons cornstarch
1 tablespoon soy sauce
1 teaspoon salt
1 egg white
1 cup vegetable oil

Grind the fish, shrimp and bacon through the fine blade of a food chopper, or chop very fine. Mix in the nuts, cornstarch, soy sauce, salt, egg white and 1 tablespoon oil until thoroughly blended. Form heaping tablespoons of the mixture into flat patties.

Heat the remaining oil in a skillet until it bubbles. Fry the patties in it until browned on both sides. Serve hot.

Makes about 24.

JAPANESE PORK-STUFFED CLAMS

24 cherrystone clams
½ pound ground pork
½ cup finely chopped green onions
1 tablespoon soy sauce
2 tablespoons dry sherry

1 teaspoon sugar
1 teaspoon ground ginger
3 tablespoons vegetable oil
½ cup beef broth

Wash and scrub the clams until water runs clean. Place in a deep skillet with ½ cup water, cover and cook until shells open. Discard any clams that don't open. Drain, remove the clams and reserve the shells.

Chop the clams, then mix with the pork, green onions, soy sauce, sherry, sugar and ginger. Divide the mixture among the shells. Combine the oil and broth in a baking pan; arrange the clams in it in a single layer. Bake in a 350° oven 20 minutes.

Makes 24.

PICKLED CLAMS, ITALIAN STYLE

36 littleneck clams	¼ teaspoon freshly ground black
½ cup olive oil	pepper
½ cup chopped onions	1 cup white wine vinegar
1 clove garlic, minced	1 cup dry white wine
6 anchovies, minced	¼ cup chopped parsley

Wash and scrub the clams under cold running water until water runs clear. Heat the oil in a deep large saucepan; sauté the onions and garlic 5 minutes. Mix in the anchovies and pepper and add the clams, vinegar and wine. Bring to a boil, cover and cook over low heat 5 minutes, or until the shells open. Discard any that do not open. Remove the clams and cook the stock over high heat 5 minutes.

Discard the clam shells. Put the clams in a bowl and strain the stock over them. Add parsley. Cool, cover and keep in the refrigerator at least 12 hours before serving. Drain and pierce with cocktail picks.

Makes 36.

JAPANESE SAUTÉED CLAMS

¼ cup condensed black bean soup	3 tablespoons sugar
½ cup dry sherry	24 shucked clams
½ cup soy sauce	4 tablespoons vegetable oil
½ teaspoon powdered ginger	

In a saucepan mix together until smooth the soup, sherry, soy sauce, ginger and sugar. Bring to a boil, remove from the heat and marinate the clams in the mixture 15 minutes. Drain, reserving the marinade.

Heat the oil in a skillet; sauté the clams 5 minutes, shaking the pan frequently. Pierce with cocktail picks and serve with the reserved heated marinade, as a dip.

Makes 24.

CLAMS DELMONICO

¼ pound sweet butter
1 teaspoon salt
2 teaspoons minced garlic
1 tablespoon lemon juice
3 tablespoons chopped pimiento
36 cherrystone clams
¾ pound lump crab meat

Cream the butter and blend in the salt, garlic, lemon juice and pimiento.

Open the clams and loosen the clams from the shell. Cover the clams on the shell with the crab meat and then spread a little of the butter mixture over the crab meat. Broil for 5 minutes or until butter melts and top is delicately browned.

Makes 36.

ALMEJAS FRITOS (Fried Clams, Spanish Style)

36 shucked littleneck or cherrystone clams
1 cup milk
½ cup dry bread crumbs
½ cup flour
Fat for deep frying
¼ pound (1 stick) butter
⅛ teaspoon Tabasco
2 tablespoons minced parsley

Soak the clams in the milk for 10 minutes. Drain well and roll in a mixture of the bread crumbs and flour. Heat the fat to 370° and fry a few clams at a time until browned. Drain.

Melt the butter and stir in the Tabasco and parsley. Serve in a small dish as a dip.

Makes 36.

CLAM CAKES

1 10½-ounce can minced clams
1½ cups sifted flour
½ teaspoon salt
1½ teaspoons baking powder
1 egg
¼ teaspoon freshly ground black
  pepper

1 tablespoon grated onions
½ cup milk
2 tablespoons melted butter
½ cup vegetable oil

Drain the clams, reserving the liquid.

Sift the flour, salt and baking powder into a bowl. Beat the egg, then mix in the pepper, onions, clam liquid, milk and melted butter. Add to the flour mixture, beating until smooth. Mix in the clams.

Heat the oil in a skillet until it bubbles. Drop the clam mixture into it by the heaping teaspoon. Fry until browned on both sides. Drain. Pierce with cocktail picks.

Makes about 36.

CLAM FRITTER HORS D'OEUVRE

1 10½-ounce can minced clams
1 egg yolk
½ cup sifted flour
¼ teaspoon salt
⅛ teaspoon white pepper

1 tablespoon grated onions
1 teaspoon olive oil
1 egg white, stiffly beaten
Vegetable oil for deep frying

Drain the clams, reserving ¼ cup liquid. Chop fine. Beat the egg yolk and clam juice together. Mix in the flour, salt, pepper, onions and olive oil. Fold in the egg white, then the clams. Let stand 1 hour.

Heat the oil to 375°. Drop teaspoons of the mixture into it. Fry until browned on all sides, about 5 minutes. Drain; pierce with cocktail picks. Serve hot with tartar sauce or chili sauce.

Makes about 24.

CLAM COCKTAIL FRITTERS

1 7-ounce can minced clams
Milk
1 envelope potato pancake mix
2 tablespoons minced onions

1 egg
2 tablespoons minced parsley
1 cup vegetable oil

Drain the clams; reserve and measure the juice. Add enough milk to make 1 cup.

Blend together the pancake mix, onions, liquid, egg and parsley. Let stand 10 minutes, then stir in the clams. Heat the oil until it bubbles. Drop the clam mixture into it by the teaspoon. Fry until browned on both sides. Drain, pierce with cocktail picks and serve hot.

Makes about 36.

VONGOLE GRATINATE (Italian Baked Clams)

36 hard-shell clams
¼ cup finely chopped parsley
2 cloves garlic, minced
¼ cup grated Parmesan cheese
¼ teaspoon freshly ground black
    pepper

½ teaspoon orégano
¼ cup olive oil
¼ cup dry bread crumbs

Scrub the clams under cold running water until shells are shiny. Dry, then place in a skillet. Cover and place over low heat until shells open. Discard the top shells. Arrange the clams on the half shell in a baking dish. Sprinkle with a mixture of the parsley, garlic, cheese, pepper and orégano, then sprinkle with the oil and finally the bread crumbs. Bake in a 425° oven 5 minutes. Serve immediately.

Makes 36.

LOBSTER RUMAKI, JAPANESE STYLE

2 raw African lobster tails
½ cup soy sauce
¼ cup dry sherry

Water chestnuts
Bacon slices

Thaw the lobster tails and remove the raw meat. Cut crosswise into ¼-inch slices. Marinate in a mixture of the soy sauce and sherry 30 minutes. Drain.

Wrap a lobster slice and a water chestnut in a slice of bacon and secure with a toothpick. Arrange on a rack in a pan and bake in a 400° oven 15 minutes or until the bacon is crisp.

Makes about 18.

OYSTERS ROCKEFELLER, NEW ORLEANS FASHION

2 dozen oysters on the half shell
Rock salt or foil
4 tablespoons chopped green onions
1/4 pound raw spinach
4 tablespoons chopped parsley
6 drops Tabasco

1/2 teaspoon salt
1/8 teaspoon freshly ground black
  pepper
1/2 cup dry bread crumbs
4 tablespoons melted butter

Loosen the oysters from the shells but leave in the shells. Fill a baking pan with rock salt or flattened crumpled foil. Heat the pan in a 450° oven while preparing the oysters. Chop together the green onions, spinach, parsley, Tabasco, salt and pepper. Mix together the bread crumbs and butter. Arrange the oysters on the half shell on the rock salt or foil.

Bake the oysters until the edges curl, remove from the oven and quickly spread each oyster with some of the spinach mixture. Sprinkle with the bread crumbs. Return to oven and bake 5 minutes longer. Serve at once.

Makes 24.

HUÎTRES AU GRATIN (Baked Oysters with Cheese, French Style)

36 oysters on the half shell
1 tablespoon flour
3/4 cup bottled clam juice
3 tablespoons heavy cream
4 tablespoons butter
1 tablespoon dry vermouth

2 egg yolks
1 tablespoon lemon juice
1/4 teaspoon white pepper
3/4 cup grated Gruyère or Swiss
  cheese

Drain the oysters, reserving the juice. Wash and dry the shells. Cook the oysters in the juice until the edges curl. Remove and drain, reserving the juices.

Mix together the flour, clam juice, cream and oyster juices. Cook over low heat, stirring steadily to the boiling point. Mix in the butter and vermouth; cook over low heat 5 minutes. Beat the egg yolks, lemon juice and pepper in a bowl; gradually add the hot sauce, stirring steadily to prevent curdling. Divide half the sauce among the shells; place an oyster in each shell and cover with the remaining sauce. Sprinkle with the cheese; place under a hot broiler until browned.

Makes 36.

ANGELS ON HORSEBACK, ENGLISH STYLE

24 shucked oysters
Freshly ground black pepper
Paprika
24 slices bacon

Sprinkle the oysters with pepper and paprika. Wrap a slice of bacon around each and fasten with a toothpick. Arrange on a rack in a pan and bake in a 375° oven 10 minutes, or until the bacon is browned and crisp. Serve hot.
Makes 24.

Note: Clams may be prepared in the same manner.

HUÎTRES À LA CRÈME (Oysters Baked in Cream, French Style)

24 oysters on the half shell
1 cup heavy cream
1 cup grated Parmesan cheese
½ cup melted butter

Gently loosen the oyster from the shell. Replace in the shells and pour over each oyster 2 teaspoons cream. Sprinkle each with 2 teaspoons cheese and 1 teaspoon butter. Put under a hot broiler until edges of oysters curl and cheese is lightly browned.
Makes 24.

BAKED SHERRIED OYSTERS

36 oysters on the half shell
4 teaspoons flour
½ cup heavy cream
¼ cup bottled clam juice
4 tablespoons butter
4 tablespoons dry sherry

2 egg yolks
⅛ teaspoon Tabasco
1 tablespoon lemon juice
1 cup (¼ pound) grated Swiss cheese

Remove the oysters from shells reserving the juice; wash and dry the shells. Place oysters and juice in a skillet and cook over low heat 2 minutes or until the edges curl. Drain the oysters, reserving the juice.

Blend the flour with cream, clam juice and oyster juice and cook over low heat, stirring, until the boiling point. Blend in the butter and sherry and cook 5 minutes longer. Beat the egg yolks with the Tabasco and lemon juice and gradually add the hot sauce, stirring steadily to prevent curdling. Divide half the sauce among the oyster shells, put an oyster on each and cover with remaining sauce. Sprinkle tops with the cheese and place under a hot broiler until browned.

Makes 36.

BROCHETTE D'HUÎTRES ET CHAMPIGNONS (Oysters and Mushrooms en Brochette, French Style)

24 shucked oysters
1 tablespoon lemon juice
24 mushroom caps
12 slices bacon, cut in half
3 tablespoons melted butter

Sprinkle the oysters with the lemon juice. Use 24 skewers or toothpicks and on each, place a mushroom cap. Run the skewer through one end of the bacon, then an oyster. Wind the bacon around the oyster and pierce with the skewer again. Brush with the melted butter and broil until bacon is browned, turning the skewers several times to brown all sides. Serve with lemon wedges.

Makes 24.

SCALLOPS EN BROCHETTE

1 pound scallops
½ teaspoon salt
⅛ teaspoon freshly ground black pepper
8 slices bacon, cut in half
3 tablespoons butter, melted

Wash and dry the scallops thoroughly. If sea scallops are used, cut in half crosswise; leave bay scallops whole. Sprinkle with the salt and pepper.

On each of 16 small skewers or toothpicks, intertwine a

half strip of bacon with 3 pieces of sea scallops or whole bay scallops. Brush the scallops with the melted butter.

Broil in a preheated broiler 3 inches from the source of heat 8 minutes, turning the skewers once.

Makes 16.

SCALLOPS IN SOY SAUCE, CHINESE STYLE

1 pound scallops
¾ cup soy sauce
¼ cup dry sherry
3 tablespoons sugar
1 clove garlic, minced
½ teaspoon powdered ginger

Wash and drain the scallops. If sea scallops are used, cut in half; leave bay scallops whole.

In a saucepan combine the soy sauce, sherry, sugar, garlic and ginger. Bring to a boil and add the scallops. Cook over high heat 7 minutes. Drain, if any liquid remains, and pierce the scallops with cocktail picks.

Makes about 30.

SCALLOP SEVICHE, CHILEAN STYLE

1 pound scallops
1 cup lime or lemon juice
¼ cup chopped green onions
¼ cup chopped pimiento
¼ cup olive oil
¾ teaspoon salt
¼ teaspoon freshly ground black pepper

If bay scallops are used, leave them whole. Cut sea scallops in quarters. Wash, drain and dry. Marinate the scallops in the lime juice 1 hour in the refrigerator, turning them occasionally. Drain. Toss with the green onions, pimiento, oil, salt and pepper. Serve with cocktail picks.

Makes about 2½ cups.

Note: The scallops are "cooked" by the action of the lime juice.

JAPANESE EGG ROLL

1 7-ounce can tuna fish
2 teaspoons sugar
6 eggs
¼ cup bottled clam juice
2 tablespoons sake or dry sherry

2 tablespoons soy sauce
½ teaspoon salt
¼ teaspoon powdered ginger
3 tablespoons vegetable oil

Drain the tuna fish and chop to a paste with the sugar. Beat together all the remaning ingredients but the oil until frothy. Blend in the tuna fish.

Heat a little of the oil in a 7-inch skillet until it bubbles. Pour in about 3 tablespoons of the mixture, turning the pan quickly to coat the bottom with a thin layer. Bake until delicately browned on both sides. Turn out onto a napkin and roll up like a jelly roll. Add oil to the pan as needed and make more pancakes with the remaining mixture. Cut in 1-inch slices and serve at room temperature.

Makes about 48 slices.

CHINESE SEAFOOD CAKES

1 pound white-meat fish
½ pound raw shrimp, shelled and deveined
¼ cup chopped green onions
1 slice salt pork
1 cup ground blanched almonds

¾ teaspoon salt
¼ teaspoon white pepper
1 tablespoon soy sauce
1 tablespoon cornstarch
1 cup vegetable oil

Wash and dry the fish and shrimp. Chop or grind very fine with the green onions, salt pork and almonds. Mix in the salt, pepper, soy sauce, cornstarch and 1 tablespoon of the oil. Using 2 tablespons, shape the mixture into round cakes.

Heat the remaining oil in a skillet; fry the cakes in it until browned on both sides. Drain and serve hot.

Makes about 24.

SILD I FLØDE (Herring in Cream Sauce, Danish Style)

6 fillets of salt herring (3 herrings)
2 cups milk
2 cups thinly sliced onions
1 cup white vinegar
¼ cup water

2 teaspoons sugar
2 teaspoons pickling spice
2 bay leaves
1 cup sour cream

Soak the herring in cold water for 4 hours; drain. Soak in the milk 2 hours. Drain.

Cut the herring into 1-inch pieces. In a glass jar or bowl, arrange alternate layers of herring and onions. Bring the vinegar, water, sugar, pickling spice and bay leaves to a boil. Cool, mix in the sour cream and pour over the herring. Cover tightly and shake. Place in the refrigerator for 2 days before serving. The herring will keep in the refrigerator for a week.

Makes about 36.

QUICK HERRING IN CREAM SAUCE

2 5-ounce jars Bismarck herring
1 cup sour cream
1 teaspoon sugar

1 cup thinly sliced onions
½ teaspoon pickling spice

Drain the herring and reserve the juice. Cut each herring in 1-inch pieces. Mix together the juice, sour cream and sugar. In a jar or bowl, arrange layers of the herring and onions, sprinkled with the pickling spice. Pour the sour-cream mixture over all. Cover and keep in the refrigerator 48 hours before serving. Keeps about 2 weeks.

Makes about 18.

MEAT AND POULTRY

As PREVIOUSLY remarked, the American palate tends toward meat. If given a choice, the vast majority of Americans would automatically select a main course of meat, perhaps poultry. This tendency has the effect of limiting our menus and cutting down the variety and interest in a well-conceived meal, especially a dinner party.

There are always intrepid hostesses who seek to deviate from the routine and the monotonous, and who may somewhat daringly serve fish or shellfish dishes for the main course. If this is done, the hors d'oeuvre should surely be of the meat type, as a sort of compensation to born meat lovers, and also to offer contrast in taste and texture for the fish or shellfish main course to follow. Needless to say, if the main course is to be beef, it would not be advisable to serve an hors d'euvre made of beef, for this would be repetitious.

Of course, if the hors d'oeuvres are served at a cocktail party, this caution would be unnecessary. At such a party, where perhaps a half-dozen hors d'oeuvres are offered, at least one should be of meat and one of poultry. Variety is especially important in a large gathering, for there are always differences in taste and personal choice, and a good selection should be available to satisfy every preference.

Most people are familiar with Chinese-style barbecued pork, a delicious and aromatic hors d'oeuvre. Korean pork is similar, but sweeter in taste, rather than spicy, and prepared with sesame seeds. Tariyaki, steak on skewers, is a Hawaiian appetizer, but of Japanese inspiration; it is excellent both for cocktail parties and as a first course for dinners. Purely Japanese, however, is rumaki, made with chicken livers, water chestnuts and bacon.

SIKH KEBOB (Indian Kebobs)

1½ pounds boneless lamb or beef
½ cup chopped onions
2 cloves garlic, minced
1 teaspoon salt
1 teaspoon turmeric
½ teaspoon powdered ginger
1 cup yogurt
2 tablespoons lemon juice
¼ cup melted butter

Cut the meat in ¼-inch cubes. Pound or chop the onions and garlic very fine, then mix with the salt, turmeric, ginger, yogurt and lemon juice. Marinate the meat in the mixture 3 hours at room temperature, basting frequently. Drain and thread 3 or 4 pieces on small skewers or toothpicks. Broil 10 minutes, basting with the butter and turning the skewers to brown all sides. Serve hot.

Makes about 24.

SIS KEBABI (Shish Kabob, Turkish Style)

2 pounds boneless lamb
1 cup dry red wine
2 teaspoons A.1. Sauce
1 clove garlic, minced
½ teaspoon freshly ground black
  pepper
½ teaspoon thyme

½ teaspoon orégano
½ cup minced parsley
2 green peppers, cut in ½-inch
  squares
16 mushrooms, cut in half
12-16 small white onions, cut in
  half

Cut the lamb in ½-inch cubes. In a bowl, combine the wine, A.1. Sauce, garlic, pepper, thyme, orégano and parsley. Marinate the lamb in the mixture 12 hours, basting and turning the meat a few times.

When ready to cook, drain the lamb, reserving the marinade. Use 16 small skewers, and on them thread the lamb, green peppers, mushrooms and onions, starting and ending with the lamb. Broil in the broiler or over charcoal, to desired degree of rareness. Turn frequently and baste with the marinade.

Makes 16.

BARBECUED PORK, CHINESE STYLE

2 pork tenderloins (about 2 pounds)
2/3 cup soy sauce
¼ cup dry sherry
2 cloves garlic, minced

2 green onions, chopped
4 slices ginger root
3 tablespoons honey
1 tablespoon sugar

If pork tenderloin is not available, buy a pork butt or boneless loin of pork and cut lengthwise into 2-inch-wide strips.

Combine the soy sauce, sherry, garlic, green onions and ginger root. Marinate the meat in the mixture 12 hours or overnight. Drain. Rub pork strips with a mixture of the honey and sugar. Place on a greased rack and roast in a 375° oven 20 minutes. Reduce heat to 300° and roast 20 minutes longer, turning the meat once. Slice and serve hot or cold, with mustard.

Makes about 48 slices.

TON YUK KUI (Marinated Pork with Sesame Seeds, Korean Style)

2 fillets of pork (about 2 pounds)	½ teaspoon black pepper
¾ cup soy sauce	1 teaspoon ground ginger
5 tablespoons sugar	2 cloves garlic
¼ cup beef broth	½ cup sesame seeds

Trim the pork of all fat. (If tenderloins are not available, loin of pork, boned and cut in long narrow strips, may be used.)

In a bowl, combine the soy sauce, sugar, broth, pepper, ginger, garlic and sesame seeds. Marinate the pork in the mixture for 3 hours at room temperature. Turn and baste the meat frequently. Drain and place on a baking pan. Roast in a 350° oven 45 minutes, turning and basting meat frequently with the marinade. Cut in ¼-inch slices.

Makes about 48 slices.

CARNITAS (Fried Pork Bits, Spanish Style)

2 pounds fat pork	½ teaspoon dried ground chili
1½ cups water	peppers
2 teaspoons salt	¼ teaspoon ground cumin

Be sure the pork is very fat. Cut the pork in ½-inch cubes. Combine in a skillet with the water, salt, chili peppers and cumin. Bring to a boil, cover and cook over high heat until the water is evaporated. Remove cover and cook pork over high heat until browned and crisp. Pierce with cocktail picks and serve with a spicy sauce as a dip, if desired.

Makes about 24.

CHINESE BARBECUED SPARERIBS

2 racks spareribs	1/3 cup soy sauce
2 tablespoons sugar	1 cup beef broth
1/3 cup honey	2 cloves garlic, minced
¼ cup cider vinegar	1 teaspoon powdered ginger

Trim all the fat off the spareribs and cut into individual ribs. Mix together all the remaining ingredients; marinate

176

the ribs in the mixture for 2 hours at room temperature, basting and turning frequently. Remove the ribs from the marinade and arrange on a rack in a baking pan. Bake in a 350° oven 45 minutes, basting frequently with the marinade. Or grill over a charcoal fire for 30 minutes. Serve hot.

SPARERIBS WITH PLUM SAUCE, SHANGHAI STYLE

3 pounds lean spareribs	1/3 cup brown sugar
1 16-ounce can green plums	1 tablespoon cornstarch
1/3 cup finely chopped crystallized ginger	¼ cup vinegar
½ cup soy sauce	1 clove garlic, minced

Cook the spareribs in salted water to cover 50 minutes or until tender. Cut the meat from the bones and into strips about 1 inch long.

Drain and mash the plums, discarding the pits. Mix with 2 tablespoons of the ginger and turn into a small bowl.

Mix together the soy sauce, sugar, cornstarch, vinegar, garlic and remaining ginger. Coat the meat with the mixture thoroughly.

Arrange the strips in a broiling pan and place the pan on the middle shelf of the broiler. Broil until browned on both sides, watching carefully to prevent burning. Pierce with cocktail picks to serve hot, or chill overnight and serve cold. Arrange around the bowl of plum sauce.

Makes about 36.

KAH-REE KUI (Korean Broiled Spareribs)

1 rack spareribs	2 tablespoons cornstarch
¼ cup dry sherry	¼ cup chopped green onions
½ cup soy sauce	1 clove garlic, minced
2 tablespoons honey	¾ cup sesame seeds
2 tablespoons sugar	

Have the rack of spareribs cut in half crosswise, and then into individual ribs. Marinate the ribs in a mixture of the sherry, soy sauce, honey, sugar, cornstarch, green onions and garlic for 2 hours at room temperature. Drain and dip each rib in the sesame seeds. Arrange the ribs on a rack in a broiling pan and broil 10 minutes on each side, or until cooked through. Serve hot.

MANDOO (Korean Dumplings)

3 cups flour
1 teaspoon salt
1 cup water
1 cup diced cooked pork
½ cup bean sprouts
½ cup diced water chestnuts

¼ cup chopped green onions
¼ cup chopped watercress
2 tablespoons soy sauce
½ teaspoon dried ground chili peppers
½ cup vegetable oil

Sift the flour and salt into a bowl; mix in the water until a firm dough is formed. Knead for a few minutes on a lightly floured surface; form into a ball and cover with a bowl. Let stand 30 minutes.

Mix together the pork, bean sprouts, water chestnuts, green onions, watercress, soy sauce and chili peppers. Taste for seasoning. Roll out the dough as thin as possible. Cut into 3-inch squares or rounds. Place a heaping teaspoon of the mixture on each and fold the dough over, sealing the edges with a little water. Cook in boiling salted water 10 minutes. Drain and brown lightly in hot oil. Serve hot.

Makes about 36.

GROUND MEAT KEBOBS

1½ pounds ground beef or lamb
1 cup minced onions
1 clove garlic, minced
1½ teaspoons salt
½ teaspoon freshly ground black pepper

1 teaspoon turmeric
1 teaspoon powdered cumin
½ teaspoon powdered ginger
1 cup yogurt
1/3 cup flour
6 tablespoons butter

Mix together the meat, onions, garlic, salt, pepper, turmeric, cumin, ginger and half the yogurt until well blended. Shape into sausages 2 inches long and ½ inch thick. Dip in the remaining yogurt, then roll in the flour.

Melt half the butter in a skillet; fry just enough of the kebobs at a time without crowding the pan, until browned on all sides. Keep hot while preparing the balance and add butter as needed. Serve hot.

Makes about 36.

TARIYAKI (Skewered Steak, Hawaiian Style)

2 pounds sirloin steak, cut ½ inch thick	4 tablespoons brown sugar
1 cup soy sauce	2 teaspoons grated onions
1/3 cup dry sherry	1 garlic clove, minced
1½ teaspoons powdered ginger	Canned pineapple chunks
	Mushroom caps, quartered

Cut the steak in ½-inch squares. Mix together the soy sauce, sherry, ginger, brown sugar, onions and garlic. Marinate the steak in the mixture for 3 hours. Drain. Thead the steak, pineapple and mushrooms on 16 small skewers or toothpicks, starting and ending with the steak. Broil 4 minutes or to desired degree of rareness, turning the skewers to brown all sides.

Makes 16.

BEEF SANDWICH APPETIZERS, PALERMO STYLE

1 12–16-inch loaf French bread	½ teaspoon freshly ground black pepper
¼ cup butter	¼ cup sour cream
1 clove garlic, minced	3 tablespoons finely chopped onions
¾ pound lean ground beef	2 tablespoons chopped capers
1 egg, beaten	
1 teaspoon salt	

Cut the bread in half lengthwise and scoop out the soft part. Spread with a mixture of the softened butter and garlic. Place on a pan and bake in a 400° oven 5 minutes or until browned.

Mix together the raw beef, egg, salt, pepper, sour cream, onions and capers. Heap on half the bread and cover with the other half. Wrap in aluminum foil and chill 2 hours. Slice thin to serve.

Makes about 20.

RICE-MEAT CROQUETTES

2½ cups chicken broth
1 cup raw rice
1 cup minced cooked meat, chicken or turkey
½ cup grated Parmesan cheese
Dash cayenne pepper

3 tablespoons minced parsley
2 eggs
½ cup flour
½ cup dry bread crumbs
Vegetable oil for deep frying

Bring the broth to a boil and add the rice. Cover and cook over low heat 20 minutes, or until tender and dry. Cool, then stir in the meat, cheese, cayenne pepper, parsley and 1 beaten egg. Form into 1-inch balls or rolls. Roll in the flour and chill 1 hour. Beat the remaining egg with a little water; dip the balls in it, then roll in the bread crumbs.

Heat the fat to 380°. Fry a few balls at a time until browned. Drain and serve with a sauce, if desired.

Makes about 24.

BACON-WRAPPED FRANKFURTERS

24 cocktail frankfurters
3 tablespoons prepared mustard
3 tablespoons chili sauce

24 pieces American cheese (⅛ by ⅛ by ¼-inch)
12 slices bacon, cut in half

Slit frankfurters lengthwise carefully so as not to cut through. Mix mustard and chili sauce together and spread inside frankfurters. Place a piece of cheese in each. Wrap a half slice of bacon around each, and fasten with toothpicks.

Arrange on a rack in a shallow pan and bake in a 375° oven 10 minutes or until the bacon is crisp.

Makes 24.

COCKTAIL FRANKFURTERS IN WINE SAUCE

2 tablespoons butter
¼ cup minced onions
1 tablespoon flour
¾ cup dry sherry

½ teaspoon salt
¼ teaspoon thyme
½ cup chili sauce
3 dozen cocktail frankfurters

Melt the butter in a saucepan; sauté the onions 3 minutes. Blend in the flour, then add the wine, stirring steadily to the boiling point. Mix in the salt, thyme and chili sauce.

Brown the frankfurters in a skillet. Drain and add to the sauce. Cook over low heat 5 minutes. Serve in a casserole to keep hot, with cocktail picks for spearing.

Makes 36.

BREADED CHICKEN CUBES

2 whole chicken breasts	¾ cup dry bread crumbs
¼ cup olive oil	¼ cup grated Parmesan cheese
1 tablespoon lemon juice	2 teaspoons minced parsley
¾ teaspoon salt	2 eggs, beaten
¼ teaspoon freshly ground black pepper	½ cup flour
½ teaspoon orégano	Vegetable oil for deep frying

Remove the skin and bones of the raw chicken breasts. Cut the chicken into small cubes. Marinate in a mixture of the oil, lemon juice, salt, pepper and orégano for 1 hour. Turn several times. Drain. Dip in a mixture of the bread crumbs, cheese and parsley, then the eggs and finally the flour.

Heat the oil to 365°. Fry the cubes in it until browned on all sides. Drain and pierce with cocktail picks. Serve hot. If not to be served immediately, keep hot in the oven.

BROCHETTES DE FOIE DE VOLAILLE (Chicken Livers on Skewers, French Style)

24 chicken livers	24 slices bacon
Salt	24 mushrooms
Pepper	¼ cup melted butter

Wash the livers in cold water, removing any discolored areas. Cut in half and season with a little salt and pepper. Cut the bacon in half crosswise and wrap around the livers. Cut the mushrooms in half; sprinkle with a little salt and pepper. Use 12 skewers and thread the livers and mushrooms on them alternately. Brush with the butter. Broil until browned, turning the skewers frequently.

Makes 12.

RUMAKI (Japanese Liver Skewers)

6 chicken livers
18 water chestnuts
9 slices bacon, cut in half crosswise

½ cup soy sauce
½ teaspoon powdered ginger

Cut each liver into 3 pieces; fold each piece around a water chestnut. Wrap a piece of bacon around the liver and chestnuts and fasten in place with a toothpick. Marinate in the soy sauce mixed with the ginger for 1 hour. Place on a rack in a shallow pan and bake in a 425° oven 10 minutes or until bacon is browned and crisp. Remove toothpicks and pierce with cocktail picks or fresh toothpicks. Serve with mashed chutney or Chinese duk sauce as a dip.

Makes 18.

LIVER BALLS AND BACON, GERMAN STYLE

1 pound chicken livers
2 hard-cooked eggs
¼ cup grated onions
1 teaspoon salt
¼ teaspoon freshly ground black pepper

2 tablespoons soft butter
1 teaspoon dry sherry
10 slices bacon, cut in half crosswise

Cook the chicken livers in boiling water for 5 minutes. Drain.

Purée the livers and hard-cooked eggs in an electric blender or force through a food mill. Blend in the onions, salt, pepper, butter and sherry. Chill. Shape into small balls and wrap a piece of bacon around each ball. Use more bacon, if needed. Fasten with toothpicks. Broil until the bacon is crisp, turning to brown all sides. Drain. Serve hot.

Makes about 20.

CURRIED CHICKEN WINGS, SIAMESE STYLE

12 chicken wings
1½ cups chopped onions
2 cloves garlic, minced
1 teaspoon salt
¼ teaspoon freshly ground black pepper

1 tablespoon curry powder
½ cup yogurt
4 tablespoons butter

Wash the wings, discard the wing tips and separate the joints. Chop or pound the onions and garlic to a paste. Mix in the salt, pepper, curry powder and yogurt. Marinate the wings in the mixture 1 hour at room temperature, basting and turning frequently.

Melt the butter in a baking pan. Arrange the wings in it. Bake in a 375° oven 30 minutes, turning the wings once to brown both sides. Serve hot.

Makes 24.

POULET À LA CIRCASSIENNE (Chicken with Walnut Sauce, Russian Style)

4 slices white bread, trimmed	1 teaspoon salt
1 cup chicken broth	⅛ teaspoon cayenne pepper
2 tablespoons butter	18 slices cold chicken or turkey
½ cup chopped onions	9 slices toast trimmed and cut in
2 cups ground walnuts	half

Soak the bread in the broth, and mash smooth.

Melt the butter in a skillet; sauté the onions until soft and golden; then mash. Gradually add the mashed bread to the walnuts, then the salt, cayenne and mashed onions. The sauce should be about the consistency of mayonnaise. If too thick, add a little more chicken broth. Arrange the chicken on the toast and cover with the sauce.

Makes 18.

YAKITORI (Japanese Chicken Skewers)

2 whole chicken breasts	3 tablespoons sugar
½ pound chicken livers	2 tablespoons grated onions
1/3 cup soy sauce	Powdered ginger
1/3 cup dry sherry	

Remove the skin and bones of the chicken and cut in bite-size pieces. Wash the livers, removing any discolored spots and cut into pieces the same size as the chicken. Using 16 small skewers or toothpicks, alternate pieces of chicken and liver.

In a saucepan, bring to a boil the soy sauce, sherry, sugar

and onions. Marinate the skewered ingredients in the mixture 15 minutes. Remove from the marinade and arrange on an oiled broiling pan. Broil 10 minutes, basting with the reserved marinade and turning frequently to brown all sides. Sprinkle with ginger and serve hot.

Makes 16.

BOULETTES DIABLES (Fried Spicy Chicken Balls, French Style)

1½ cups finely chopped cooked chicken
¼ cup minced green onions
2 tablespoons minced parsley
3 tablespoons prepared mustard
1 tablespoon curry powder

3 tablespoons ground nuts
1 cup dry bread crumbs
2 eggs
3 tablespoons cream
Vegetable oil for deep frying

Mix together the chicken, green onions, parsley, mustard, curry powder and nuts. Taste for seasoning. Shape the mixture into marble-sized balls. If mixture is too dry to hold together, add a little cream. Roll in the bread crumbs, the egg yolks beaten with the cream, and then again in the bread crumbs. Chill 2 hours.

Heat the oil to 375°. Fry the balls until browned, about 1 minute. Drain and serve hot.

Makes about 40.

VEGETABLES

MANY FOREIGN cuisines place a great deal of emphasis on vegetables as an hors d'oeuvre, as indeed they should. They provide a light, appetizing form of cocktail accompaniment or first course.

The Italians create marvelous appetizers with peppers, mushrooms and eggplant, but other countries are equally imaginative. The Greeks have a very delicious eggplant salad which is served as an appetizer alone, or as part of an hors d'oeuvre plate. In the Middle East there are exotic stuffed grape leaves, and Middle Europe prepares a similar dish, stuffed cabbage. Vegetables are particularly good for hors d'oeuvres, and even those who won't eat them when served as a vegetable course will delight in them in appetizer form.

CRUDITÉS (Raw Vegetables, French Style)

Select a variety of crisp chilled fresh vegetables such as celery stalks, carrot sticks, cauliflower flowerets, Belgian endive, artichoke leaves, radish roses, green and red pepper sticks, tiny plum tomatoes and small mushrooms. Arrange them attractively around a dip.

PICKLED CARROT STICKS, ITALIAN STYLE

12 carrots, cut in quarters lengthwise
2/3 cup olive oil
1/3 cup wine vinegar
1½ teaspoons salt

½ teaspoon freshly ground black pepper
1 teaspoon orégano
2 cloves garlic, minced

Cook the carrots in boiling salted water 10 minutes. Drain. Bring to a boil the oil, vinegar, salt, pepper, orégano and garlic. Pour over the carrots; marinate in the refrigerator at least 24 hours before serving. Drain.

Makes 48 sticks.

VEGETARIAN APPETIZER

4 tablespoons vegetable oil
1½ pounds mushrooms, sliced
1 cup diced onions
2 hard-cooked eggs

1½ teaspoons salt
½ teaspoon freshly ground black pepper

Heat the oil in a skillet. Sauté the mushrooms and onions 10 minutes.

Chop the mushrooms, onions, egg, salt and pepper together

185

until smooth. Chill. Serve on lettuce or as a cocktail spread. Makes about 3 cups.

CHOPPED EGGPLANT APPETIZER

1 2-pound eggplant
¼ cup minced onions
½ cup minced green peppers
2 tablespoons vegetable or olive oil
4 tablespoons lemon juice

1½ teaspoons salt
¼ teaspoon freshly ground black pepper
1 teaspoon sugar

Wash the eggplant, dry and wrap loosely in aluminum foil. Bake in a 475° oven 1 hour. Cool and peel.

Chop the eggplant very fine. Beat in the onions, green peppers, oil, lemon juice, salt, pepper and sugar. Chill. Serve with thinly sliced pumpernickel and black olives.

Makes about 3 cups.

CAPALATINA (Pickled Eggplant Appetizer, Sicilian Style)

2 (about 4 pounds) eggplant
1 tablespoon salt
¾ cup olive oil
1½ cups chopped onions
1 cup sliced celery
1 20-ounce can Italian-style tomatoes
1 cup pitted black olives (Italian or Greek)

¼ cup drained capers
2 tablespoons pine nuts or slivered blanched almonds
2 tablespoons sugar
¼ cup wine vinegar
½ teaspoon freshly ground black pepper

Wash and cut the unpeeled eggplant into 1-inch cubes. Place in a colander, sprinkle with the salt and let stand 1 hour, turning the eggplant several times. Press out all the liquid, then turn out onto paper towels and pat dry.

Heat the oil in a skillet; brown the eggplant cubes in it on all sides. Remove with a slotted spoon. To the oil remaining in the skillet, add the onions and celery; sauté until browned. Add the tomatoes and olives. Bring to a boil and cook over low heat 10 minutes. Add the capers, nuts, sugar, vinegar, pepper and sautéed eggplant. Bring to a boil, cover and cook over low heat 25 minutes, stirring frequently. Cool, chill and serve with thinly sliced Italian bread.

Makes about 1 quart.

CAVIAR EN TOMATE (Caviar-Stuffed Tomatoes, Russian Style)

Buy very small cherry tomatoes (love apples). Cut a thin slice off the stem end and scoop out the pulp carefully. Turn upside down to drain for a few minutes. Stuff the tomatoes with caviar. Put each tomato (cut side down) on a buttered toast round. Pipe a border of sieved egg yolk around the base of each tomato.

Tomatoes prepared in this manner may also be stuffed with avocado mixtures, Lomi Lomi, pâté, etc.

PLAKY (Armenian Bean Appetizer)

1 cup dried white beans	1 tablespoon chopped fresh dill, or
2½ cups water	⅛ teaspoon dried dill
3 tablespoons olive oil	2 cloves garlic, minced
1 carrot, sliced	1 teaspoon salt
½ cup diced onions	½ teaspoon freshly ground black
¾ cup sliced celery	pepper
2 tablespoons chopped parsley	Lemon wedges

Wash the beans, cover with water, bring to a boil, cover and let stand 1 hour. Drain. Add the 2½ cups water, bring to a boil, cover and cook over low heat 1¼ hours.

While the beans are cooking, heat the oil in a skillet; sauté the carrot, onions and celery 10 minutes. Add the parsley, dill and garlic and cook 2 minutes. Add the mixture to the beans with the salt. Cook 15 minutes longer or until the beans are tender. Add the pepper, and more salt if necessary. Mash lightly. Serve at room temperature with lemon wedges and thinly sliced French bread. Makes about 3½ cups.

ISRAELI "HOT DOGS"

1 pound dried chick peas	1¼ teaspoons salt
3 slices white bread, trimmed	¼ teaspoon pepper
2 eggs	Vegetable oil for deep frying
½ teaspoon minced garlic	
¼ teaspoon dried ground red peppers	

Wash the chick peas; cover with water, bring to a boil and soak 2 hours. Drain.

Grind the chick peas and bread in a food chopper. Mix in the eggs, garlic, red peppers, salt and pepper. Shape tablespoons of the mixture into small rolls like sausages. Chill for 1 hour.

Heat the oil to 370° and carefully drop the rolls into it. Fry until browned. Drain. Serve with mustard and relish.

Makes about 20.

CECI ALL'OLIO (Chick Peas in Garlic Oil, Italian Style)

1 can chick peas
¼ cup olive oil
2 cloves garlic, minced
1 teaspoon salt

½ teaspoon black pepper
2 teaspoons lemon juice
1 tablespoon minced parsley

Drain the chick peas very thoroughly. Heat the oil in a skillet; add the garlic and chick peas. Sauté until lightly browned. Drain well. Season with the salt, pepper, lemon juice and parsley. Serve hot or cold. Serves 4-6.

ASPARAGUS ROLLUPS

16 slices prosciutto or 8 thin slices boiled ham
16 cooked or canned asparagus
16 strips pimiento

If prosciutto is used, trim each slice evenly. Cut the boiled ham in half lengthwise. Roll up each asparagus in a piece of ham, then wrap a piece of pimiento around each. Fasten with cocktail picks. Makes 16.

TOASTED ASPARAGUS ROLLS

24 thin slices very fresh white bread
1 cup grated cheddar or Swiss cheese

24 cooked or canned asparagus
½ cup melted butter

Trim the crusts off the bread and arrange the slices on a damp towel. Cover with a piece of wax paper and gently roll

188

the bread a little thinner. Sprinkle each slice with some cheese; place an asparagus at one end and roll up like a jelly roll. Fasten with toothpicks. Arrange the rolls on a greased baking sheet and brush well with melted butter. Bake in a 400° oven 10 minutes or until delicately browned.

Makes 24.

PEPERONATA CON OLIVE (Red Peppers in Oil, Sicilian Style)

6 large sweet red peppers
1 teaspoon salt
1½ cups pitted Italian olives

3 cloves garlic, minced
½ cup olive oil

Bake the peppers in a 425° oven 20 minutes or until the skin blisters and blackens; turn occasionally.

Slip off the skins; discard the cores and seeds. Cut the peppers into narrow strips; toss with the salt, then the olives and garlic. Add the oil; let marinate at least 4 hours before serving. Turn mixture occasionally. The peppers will keep a few weeks in a tightly closed jar.

Serves 10–12.

FRENCH-FRIED MUSHROOMS

1½ pounds mushrooms
¼ cup flour
2 cups vegetable oil

Salt
Freshly ground black pepper

Wash and thoroughly dry the mushrooms. Cut in ½-inch slices, stems and all; toss with the flour. Heat the oil to 375°; fry the mushrooms 2 minutes. Drain well; sprinkle with salt and pepper. Pierce with cocktail picks and serve hot.

Makes about 30.

CURRIED MUSHROOM ROLLS

¼ pound (1 stick) butter
½ pound mushrooms, chopped
3 tablespoons minced onions
1 tablespoon lemon juice
½ teaspoon salt

⅛ teaspoon freshly ground black pepper
1 teaspoon curry powder
12 thin slices white bread

189

Melt 2 tablespoons of the butter in a skillet; sauté the mushrooms and onions 5 minutes. Mix in the lemon juice, salt, pepper and curry powder. Cook 1 minute, or until the liquid is evaporated. Taste for seasoning.

Remove the crusts of the bread. Roll each slice between two sheets of wax paper very thin. Spread lightly with some of the remaining butter. Spread about 1 tablespoon of the mushroom mixture on each slice and roll up like a jelly roll. Fasten the ends with toothpicks and arrange on a buttered baking sheet. Melt the remaining butter and brush the rolls with it. Bake in a 425° oven 8 minutes or until browned. Serve hot as a first course, or cut in ½-inch slices and serve as a hot hors d'oeuvre.

Makes 12 rolls, or about 60 hors d'oeuvres.

CHAMPIGNONS MARINÉS (Marinated Mushrooms, French Style)

1 pound small button mushrooms	¼ teaspoon freshly ground black
5 tablespoons lemon juice	pepper
4 tablespoons olive oil	2 tablespoons cognac
¼ cup minced onions	2 tablespoons minced parsley
1 teaspoon salt	

Remove mushroom stems. (Reserve for another purpose.) Wash caps in water with 1 tablespoon lemon juice. Drain and dry. Heat the oil in a skillet and sauté the onions 3 minutes. Add mushrooms and sauté 2 minutes. Stir in the remaining lemon juice, salt and pepper. Cover and cook over low heat 5 minutes. Stir in the cognac, then chill 3 hours. Serve with parsley, and surrounded by picks. Makes about 40.

CHAMPIGNONS SAUTÉS SUR CANAPÉS (Mushrooms in Champagne on Toast, French Style)

3 tablespoons butter	1 teaspoon salt
1 pound mushrooms, sliced	⅛ teaspoon freshly ground black
1 tomato, peeled and chopped	pepper
1 tablespoon chopped parsley	Toast squares
1/3 cup champagne or dry white wine	

Melt the butter in a skillet. Add the mushrooms, tomato and parsley. Sauté for 5 minutes, stirring frequently. Mix in the champagne, salt and pepper. Cook over high heat for 5 minutes, or until fairly dry, stirring frequently. Heap on the toast squares.

Makes about 24.

SHRIMP-STUFFED MUSHROOMS, CHINESE STYLE

12 Chinese dried mushrooms	1 teaspoon dry sherry
½ pound raw shrimp, shelled and deveined	1 teaspoon cornstarch
1 teaspoon salt	1 egg white
2 tablespoons minced green onions	¼ cup water
½ teaspoon ground ginger	2 tablespoons vegetable oil
	1 tablespoon soy sauce

This dish is customarily prepared with dried mushrooms, but if you can't get them, buy large firm mushrooms. Soak the dried mushrooms in lukewarm water for 30 minutes. Drain. Remove the stems of the dried or fresh mushrooms and use for another purpose.

Chop the shrimp very fine and mix with the salt, green onions, ginger, sherry, cornstarch and egg white. Stuff the mushrooms. Arrange in a skillet, stuffing up. Add a mixture of the water, oil and soy sauce. Bring to a boil, cover and cook over low heat 10 minutes. Drain. Serve hot.

Makes 12.

CHAMPIGNONS FARCIS (Mushrooms Stuffed with Liver, French Style)

18 large mushrooms
5 tablespoons butter
½ pound chicken livers
2 tablespoons minced onions
1 3-ounce package cream cheese, softened
¾ teaspoon salt
¼ teaspoon freshly ground black pepper

Wash and dry the mushrooms. Remove and chop the stems. Heat 3 tablespoons of the butter in a skillet; sauté the mushroom caps 5 minutes, turning frequently. Remove.

191

Add the remaining butter to the pan and cook the chicken livers, mushroom stems and onions 5 minutes. Chop the mixture very fine, and let cool.

Beat the cheese smooth, then mix in the liver mixture, salt and pepper. Fill the mushroom caps with the mixture and chill.

Makes 18.

CHAMPIGNONS LANGUEDOC (Stuffed Mushrooms with Foie Gras, French Style)

1 pound firm mushrooms	3 tablespoons butter
1 cup boiling water	¼ cup chopped onions
¾ teaspoon salt	¼ cup chopped ham
2 teaspoons lemon juice	½ cup dry white wine *Foie gras*

Have the mushrooms all one size. Remove stems from mushrooms. Wash stems and caps thoroughly. Chop stems. Put caps in a saucepan with the boiling water, salt, lemon juice and half the butter. Bring to a boil, cover and cook 3 minutes. Drain caps and arrange in a buttered shallow baking dish, hollow side up.

Melt the remaining butter in a skillet and sauté the onions and ham 3 minutes. Add the chopped stems and sauté 5 minutes over high heat. Mix in the wine and cook 10 minutes or until the mixture is dry. Fill mushroom caps with stuffing and top each with a thin slice of foie gras cut the same size as the mushrooms. Bake in a 425° oven 5 minutes. Pierce with cocktail picks and serve on toast rounds, if desired.

Makes about 16.

FUNGHI RIPIENI (Stuffed Mushrooms, Italian Style)

24 large firm mushrooms	3 tablespoons dry sherry
3 tablespoons butter	¼ cup peeled chopped tomatoes
4 tablespoons olive oil	1 clove garlic, minced
4 tablespoons chopped onions	2 tablespoons dry bread crumbs
1 teaspoon salt	1 tablespoon minced parsley
⅛ teaspoon freshly ground black pepper	

Wash and dry the mushrooms; remove the stems and chop them. Lightly salt the unpeeled caps.

Heat the butter and 1 tablespoon oil in a skillet; sauté the onions and chopped mushroom stems 5 minutes. Add the salt, pepper, sherry, tomatoes and garlic. Cook over high heat 3 minutes. Stir in the bread crumbs and parsley, taste for seasoning, and stuff the mushroom caps. Arrange on an oiled baking sheet; bake in a 425° oven 10 minutes, basting frequently with the remaining 3 tablespoons oil. Pierce with cocktail picks and serve hot.

Makes 24.

DOLMEH BARG (Stuffed Grape Leaves, Arabian Style)

1 can grape leaves	¼ cup lemon juice
2 cups beef broth	1 tablespoon tomato paste

Buy the grape leaves in Greek, Armenian or specialty shops. Use 40 leaves for stuffing, and the rest for lining the pan and separating the layers. Cut off the stems. Drain the leaves and cover with hot water. Drain and spread out on a flat surface. Put a tablespoon of the meat or rice filling on each leaf. Fold opposite ends towards the center, then roll up like a sausage. Cover the bottom of a heavy deep skillet with leaves and arrange the rolls in layers, separating each layer with leaves. Add a mixture of the broth, lemon juice and tomato paste. Put a plate on top to weight it down, and cover the skillet. Cook over low heat 1¼ hours or until tender.

Meat Filling:

1 pound ground beef	½ teaspoon cinnamon
1 cup half-cooked rice	½ cup chopped scallions
1½ teaspoons salt	(green onions)
½ teaspoon freshly ground black pepper	½ cup chopped parsley
	2 tablespoons melted butter

Mix all the ingredients together lightly. Proceed as directed. Serve hot, with yogurt.

Makes 40.

Rice Filling:

¾ cup olive oil
3 cups chopped onions
1¼ cups raw rice
¼ cup currants or seedless raisins
¾ cup chopped dill or parsley

1¼ teaspoons salt
½ teaspoon freshly ground black pepper
½ teaspoon ground allspice
½ cup boiling water

Heat ½ cup oil in a skillet; mix in the onions and rice. Sauté over low heat 15 minutes, stirring very frequently. Mix in the currants, dill, salt, pepper and allspice; cook 3 minutes. Add the remaining oil and water. Cover and cook over very low heat 20 minutes, or until tender. Watch carefully to prevent burning. Stuff the grape leaves and follow previous directions. Serve hot or cold. Garnish with lemon slices.

Makes 40.

MIHSHEE MALOOF (Persian Stuffed Cabbage Leaves)

1 large head cabbage
½ cup split peas
1 pound ground beef
1 cup chopped onions
½ cup chopped parsley
½ teaspoon cinnamon

2 teaspoons salt
½ teaspoon freshly ground black pepper
1½ cups beef broth
½ cup lemon juice
¼ cup sugar

Wash the cabbage, cover with water, bring to a boil and cook over low heat 15 minutes. Drain and carefully remove 24 leaves. Cook the peas in boiling water 30 minutes or until tender. Drain.

Mix together the peas, beef, onions, parsley, cinnamon, 1 teaspoon salt and ¼ teaspoon pepper. Put a heaping tablespoon of the mixture on each leaf. Fold in the opposite ends, then roll up into sausage shapes. If there is any filling left, use a few more cabbage leaves.

Line the bottom of a deep skillet with additional cabbage leaves and arrange the rolls in it, placing more leaves between the layers. Add the broth and the remaining salt and pepper, then cover with cabbage leaves. Cover the skillet and cook over low heat 30 minutes. Mix in the lemon juice and sugar. Cook 30 minutes; taste for seasoning.

Makes about 24.

FIRST COURSES

MANY PEOPLE prefer to serve one appetizer before dinner, either in the living room or at the dining room table, rather than a variety of small hors d'oeuvres. In either case the selection should be more substantial and, if served in the living room, the proper silver should be provided. Any but the most formal dinner may be preceded by a first course served in the living room. This is a particularly good method if the hostess is serving the entire meal herself. It is then possible for her to be seated at the table after serving the main course, resulting in a more relaxed hostess.

First courses may be hot or cold, but should complement the main course, so that ingredients are not repeated. If the first course has a sauce with a pronounced flavor, serve a plain roast or broiled main course.

Hors d'oeuvres which are suitable to serve as first courses at a dinner come from all over the globe. Burma features nga sok hin, fish balls in a type of curry sauce, although it will be noted that the dish is not made with packaged curry powder. From almost every country of South America, where pickled fish is popular as an appetizer, comes escabeche de pescado. For those who enjoy herring, Germany prepared a most unusual combination (Hering mit Apfeln und Zwiebeln), consisting of herring in sour cream with apples and onions. Another unusual combination, theoretically but not in practice, is Italy's fagioli toscani col tonno, tuna fish and white beans. Another apparent oddity is veal prepared with tuna fish sauce (vitello tonnato), a classic Italian appetizer. From Scandinavia comes an extremely imaginative first course, consisting of pancakes filled with smoked fish, guaranteed to win praise for any hostess who prepares it. The tiny island of Curaçao, off the coast of South America, is part of the Netherlands; here they feature an original way of stuffing a whole Edam cheese, which makes a fascinating conversation piece of a first course.

NGA SOK HIN (Fish Balls in Curry Sauce, Burma Style)

3 pounds fish fillets
¾ cup oil
2 cups finely chopped onions
3 cloves garlic, minced
2 teaspoons salt
¾ teaspoon dried ground chili
  peppers

1 teaspoon turmeric
1 teaspoon grated lemon rind
4 tablespoons cornstarch
2 cups chopped tomatoes

Grind the fish twice or chop very fine. Heat half the oil in a skillet; sauté the onions and garlic 10 minutes, stirring frequently. Mix in the salt, chili peppers, turmeric and lemon rind. Remove a little less than half of the mixture and add to the fish. Mix until smooth. Shape into walnut-size balls and roll in the cornstarch.

Add the remaining oil to the onion mixture left in the skillet; sauté the fish balls until lightly browned. Shake the skillet frequently. Add the tomatoes; cover and cook over low heat 20 minutes. Taste for seasoning. Serves 6-8.

MOUSSE DE JAMBON (Ham-Tongue Mousse, French Style)

1 tablespoon butter
3 tablespoons minced shallots or
  onions
2 envelopes (tablespoons) gelatin
1/3 cup dry sherry
2 cups hot chicken broth
¾ pound cooked ham, diced
3 tablespoons cognac

4 teaspoons tomato paste
½ teaspoon freshly ground pepper
Salt
½ pound cooked tongue, diced
  small
2 tablespoons minced dill or parsley
¾ cup heavy cream, whipped

Melt the butter in a skillet; sauté the shallots or onions 5 minutes. Sprinkle the gelatin into the sherry; let stand 5 minutes, then add the hot chicken broth, stirring until dissolved. Mix in the sautéed shallots.

Using about ½ cup of ham and ½ cup liquid at a time, blend the ham in an electric blender until very smooth. Empty bowl and continue process until all the ham is blended. Or grind the ham through the fine blade of a food chopper three times, then blend in the liquid. To the ham mixture, add the cognac, tomato paste, pepper and salt to taste. Cool until

196

mixture begins to set. Stir in the tongue, dill or parsley and whipped cream. Pack into a lightly oiled 1½-quart mold. Cover and chill overnight, or for at least 4 hours or until firm.

Unmold onto lettuce or other greens and garnish with pimientos, olives, cherry tomatoes, etc. Serve with tomato or sour-cream horseradish sauce, if desired.

Serves 6–8.

MOUSSE DE VOLAILLE (Chicken Mousse, French Style)

2 envelopes (tablespoons) gelatin	1 tablespoon finely grated onion
¼ cup cold water	1 tablespoon lemon juice
½ cup hot chicken stock	1 teaspoon salt
3 egg yolks	¼ teaspoon white pepper
1½ cups milk	1 tablespoon minced parsley
2½ cups finely chopped chicken	1 cup heavy cream

Soften the gelatin in the water for 5 minutes, then stir into the hot broth until dissolved. Beat the egg yolks in the top of a double boiler. Mix in the milk; place over hot water and cook, stirring steadily, until the mixture coats the spoon. Add the gelatin mixture, chicken, onion, lemon juice, salt, pepper and parsley. Cool. Whip the cream and fold into the chicken mixture. Turn into an oiled 1½-quart mold. Chill, then carefully turn out onto a chilled serving dish. Serve with French dressing or mayonnaise. Serves 4-6.

BLENDER SALMON MOUSSE

1 envelope (tablespoon) gelatin	½ teaspoon salt
2 tablespoons diced onions	¼ teaspoon white pepper
2 tablespoons lemon juice	2 7-ounce cans salmon, drained
½ cup boiling water	1 cup heavy cream
½ cup mayonnaise	
2 sprigs fresh dill or 1 teaspoon dried	

Combine the gelatin, onions, lemon juice and boiling water in the blender bowl. Blend at high speed for about 30 seconds.

Turn motor off; add the mayonnaise, dill, salt, pepper and salmon. Turn to high speed for about 20 seconds. Remove cover and gradually add the cream until thoroughly blended. Turn into an oiled 1-quart mold. Chill, then carefully turn out.

Serves 8.

MARINERAD LAX (Marinated Salmon, Swedish Style)

1½ cups sliced onions	½ cup white vinegar
3 cups water	1 teaspoon sugar
2 teaspoons salt	1 teaspoon pickling spice
6 slices salmon	2 bay leaves
½ cup lemon juice	¼ teaspoon whole peppercorns

Combine the onions, water and salt in a deep skillet. Bring to a boil, add the salmon and cook over low heat 45 minutes. Carefully transfer salmon to a bowl.

Mix the lemon juice, vinegar, sugar, pickling spice, bay leaves and peppercorns into the fish stock. Bring to a boil and cook 5 minutes. Pour over the fish. Cool. Let marinate in the refrigerator at least 24 hours before serving.

Serves 6.

PICKLED FISH

1½ cups chopped onions	1 cup sliced onions
6 slices pike, salmon or whitefish	½ cup white vinegar
1½ teaspoons salt	1½ tablespoons sugar
¼ teaspoon pepper	2 teaspoons pickling spice
2 cups water	2 bay leaves

Combine the chopped onions, fish, salt, pepper and water in a saucepan. Bring to a boil and cook over low heat 25 minutes. In a glass or pottery bowl, arrange alternate layers of the fish and sliced onions. Add the vinegar, sugar, pickling spice and bay leaves to the fish stock. Bring to a boil and pour over the fish. Cool, cover and refrigerate for two days before serving.

Serves 6.

ESCABECHE DE PESCADO (Pickled Fish, South American Style)

1½ pounds fish fillets (sole, mackerel, etc.)	½ teaspoon ground cumin
½ cup flour	¼ teaspoon saffron
2 teaspoons salt	1 cup wine vinegar
½ cup olive oil	1 cup water
3 cloves garlic, minced	2 bay leaves
	1 lemon, thinly sliced

Wash and dry the fish; cut in 2-inch lengths. Dip in a mixture of the flour and 1 teaspoon salt. Heat the oil in a skillet; brown the fish in it. Drain.

In the oil remaining in the skillet, sauté the garlic 1 minute. Mix in the cumin, saffron, then gradually add the vinegar, water and remaining salt. Bring to a boil and pour over the fish. Arrange the bay leaves and lemon over the fish. Cool, cover, then marinate in the refrigerator for 24 hours before serving. The fish will keep a week. Serve cold.

Serves 6–8.

HERING MIT APFELN UND ZWIEBELN (Herring with Apples and Onions, German Style)

8 salt herring fillets	1 cup peeled diced tart apples
2 cups sour cream	2 cups thinly sliced onions
½ cup white vinegar	6 peppercorns
1 tablespoon olive oil	1 bay leaf

Wash the herring fillets, cover with water and let soak 24 hours, changing the water several times. Drain, dry and cut in 2-inch pieces. Arrange the herring in a glass or pottery bowl. Mix together the sour cream, vinegar and oil. Fold in the apples, onions, peppercorns and bay leaf. Pour over the herring. Cover and marinate in the refrigerator at least 24 hours before serving.

Serves 8.

BRATHERINGE (Marinated Fried Herring, German Style)

6 fillets of salt herring (3 herrings)	2 tablespoons olive oil
½ cup flour	3 peppercorns
½ cup vegetable oil	¼ teaspoon mustard seed
2/3 cup vinegar	2 bay leaves
1/3 cup water	1 cup sliced onions

Soak the herring fillets in cold water 2 hours, changing the water twice. Drain and dry. Dip in the flour, coating the fillets well. Heat the vegetable oil in a skillet; brown the fillets in it on both sides. Drain and arrange in a glass or pottery dish.

Combine and bring to a boil the vinegar, water, oil, peppercorns, mustard seed and bay leaves. Cool. Spread the onions over the herring, then pour the vinegar mixture over all. Marinate in the refrigerator at least 24 hours before serving.

Serves 6–12.

RUSSIAN HERRING APPETIZER

2 5-ounce jars bismarck herring	¼ cup cider vinegar
1½ cups diced boiled potatoes	2 tablespoons water
1½ cups diced cooked or canned beets	2 tablespoons sugar
½ cup peeled diced apples	⅛ teaspoon white pepper
¼ cup chopped onions	½ cup whipped cream
¼ cup diced gherkins	2 hard-cooked eggs, sliced
	2 tablespoons chopped parsley

Rinse the herring under cold water. Drain, dry and dice. Toss with the potatoes, beets, apples, onions and gherkins.

Mix together the vinegar, water, sugar and pepper and add to the herring mixture. Fold in the whipped cream. Rinse a 1½-quart mold with cold water and pack the mixture into it. Chill 2 hours.

Turn out onto a serving dish and garnish with the hard-cooked eggs and parsley. Serves 6–8.

LEGUMI COL TONNO (Tuna-Vegetable Appetizer, Italian Style)

1 teaspoon mixed pickling spice
1 bay leaf
1 tablespoon tomato paste
3 cup water
1 cup olive oil
½ cup lemon juice
4 cloves garlic, minced
1 teaspoon salt
¼ teaspoon freshly ground black pepper
¼ teaspoon thyme

¼ teaspoon basil
1 carrot, thinly sliced
½ cup thinly sliced celery
12 small white onions, peeled
8 mushrooms, quartered
2 green peppers, thinly sliced
2 pimientos, sliced
1 dill pickle, thinly sliced
½ cup sliced green olives
½ cup sliced black olives
2 7¾-ounce cans tuna fish, drained

Tie the pickling spice and bay leaf in a cheesecloth bag. Combine in a heavy saucepan with the tomato paste, water, oil, lemon juice, garlic, salt, pepper, thyme and basil; bring to a boil. Add the carrot, celery, and onions; cook over low heat 30 minutes. Add the mushrooms and green peppers; cook 10 minutes. Add the pimientos, pickle, olives and tuna fish; cook 5 minutes longer. Discard spice bag. Cool and chill. Drain.
Serves 8–10.

FAGIOLI TOSCANI COL TONNO (Bean and Tuna Fsh Appetizer, Tuscan Style)

1½ cups dried white beans
1 clove garlic, split
2 teaspoons salt
½ cup chopped onions

½ cup olive oil
½ teaspoon freshly ground black pepper
2 7¾-ounce cans tuna fish, flaked

Wash the beans, cover with water and bring to a boil; let soak 1 hours. Drain. Add garlic and fresh water to cover. Bring to a boil and cook over low heat 2 hours or until tender, adding the salt after 1½ hours cooking time. Drain well and discard the garlic.

Toss the beans with the onions, oil and pepper. Mash lightly. Chill. Mix in the tuna.

Serves 6–8.

SHRIMP RAMEKINS

1½ pounds raw shrimp, cleaned and deveined
¼ pound butter
½ pound mushrooms, sliced
¼ pound cream cheese
1 cup sour cream

2 teaspoons salt
¼ teaspoon Tabasco
½ teaspoon paprika
2 teaspoons chopped parsley
¼ cup grated Parmesan cheese

Cut the raw shrimp in half crosswise. Melt the butter in a skillet; sauté the shrimp 2 minutes. Add the mushrooms. Cook over medium heat 5 minutes, stirring frequently.

Beat the cream cheese in a saucepan; gradually add the sour cream. Cook over low heat, stirring steadily to the boiling point. Blend in the salt, Tabasco, paprika and parsley. Fold in the shrimp. Divide mixture among 8 individual buttered ramekins or baking dishes. Sprinkle with Parmesan cheese. Place under the broiler until delicately browned.

Serves 8.

RÄKOR MED DILL (Shrimp in Lemon-Dill Butter, Swedish Style)

2 pounds raw shrimp, shelled and deveined
¼ pound (1 stick) sweet butter
1 teaspoon salt
¼ teaspoon freshly ground black pepper

1 tablespoon chopped fresh dill or 2 teaspoons dried dill
3 tablespoons lemon juice
Dash Tabasco
1 teaspoon Worcestershire sauce

Wash and dry the shrimp.

Heat the butter in a skillet; sauté the shrimp, shaking the skillet occasionally, until the shrimp are red in color, about 5 minutes. Sprinkle with the salt, pepper, dill, lemon juice,

Tabasco and Worcestershire sauce. Serve as a first course or pierce with cocktail picks and serve as a hot hors d'oeuvre.
Serves 6–8.

SHRIMP ASPIC

2 envelopes (tablespoons) gelatin
½ cup cold water
2 cups chicken broth
1 teaspoon salt
1 pound raw shrimp, shelled and deveined
2 tablespoons dry sherry

1 teaspoon lemon juice
⅛ teaspoon Tabasco
½ cup finely diced cucumbers
2 tablespoons minced onions
½ cup chopped black olives
2 tablespoons chopped pimientos

Soften the gelatin in the water. Bring the broth and salt to a boil. Add the shrimp, bring to a boil, cover and cook over low heat 3 minutes. Drain, reserving the liquid. Stir the gelatin into the hot liquid until dissolved. Add the sherry, lemon juice and Tabasco. Chill until syrupy.

Arrange a whole shrimp on the bottom of 6 individual molds. Pour a thin layer of the gelatin mixture over them and chill until set. Dice the remaining shrimp and add to the remaining gelatin mixture with the cucumbers, onions, olives and pimientos. Turn into the molds. Chill until set. Unmold onto shredded lettuce and serve with mayonnaise or Russian dressing.
Serves 6.

SHRIMP IN SHERRY-SOY SAUCE, CHINESE STYLE

1½ pounds raw shrimp, shelled and deveined
¼ cup soy sauce
¼ cup dry sherry

¼ cup vegetable oil
1 clove garlic, minced
1 teaspoon powdered ginger

Marinate the raw shrimp in a mixture of the soy sauce, sherry, oil, garlic and ginger 1 hour. Drain away all but ¼ cup of the marinade.

Put the shrimp and marinade in a skillet and cook over medium heat 5 minutes, until the shrimp are done. Serve hot.
Serves 4–6.

MOULES RAVIGOTE (Mussels with Herb Mayonnaise, French Style)

36 mussels
1 cup water
¼ cup dry white wine
1 teaspoon tarragon vinegar
4 tablespoons minced onions

2 tablespoons chopped parsley
2 tablespoons chopped capers
1 cup mayonnaise
1 hard-cooked egg white, chopped
1 teaspoon anchovy paste

Scrub the mussels with a brush under cold running water, then combine with the water in a saucepan and cook until shells open. Discard any that do not open. Cool. Remove the mussels from shells, reserving half the shells. Cut off the beard (fringe) of the mussels. Place mussels on the half shells and chill. Cook the wine, tarragon vinegar, onions, parsley and capers until liquid is reduced to half. Cool, then mix with the mayonnaise, egg white and anchovy paste. Coat the mussels with the mixture. Serve very cold.

Serves 6–8.

STUET KRABBE (Crab-Meat Ramekins, Scandinavian Style)

2 pounds lump crab meat
5 tablespoons butter
½ cup chopped onions
¾ cup diced green pepper
2 eggs
¼ cup heavy cream

2 tablespoons chopped pimientos
¾ teaspoon salt
½ teaspoon white pepper
3 tablespoons dry vermouth
2 tablespoons dry bread crumbs

Pick over the crab meat, removing any cartilage.

Melt 3 tablespoons butter in a skillet; sauté the onions and green pepper 5 minutes. Remove from the heat and cool 5 minutes. Beat the eggs with the cream; add to the sautéed vegetables with the pimientos, salt, pepper and vermouth. Mix well. Carefully fold in the crab meat. Divide the mixture among 6–8 buttered ramekins or baking dishes. Sprinkle with the bread crumbs and dot with the remaining butter. Bake in a 350° oven 15 minutes or until browned.

Serves 6–8.

CRAB-MEAT RAVIGOTE IN SHELLS

2 teaspoons dry mustard
1½ cups mayonnaise
2 tablespoons prepared horseradish
4 tablespoons chopped pimiento-
stuffed olives
2 tablespoons grated onions
3 tablespoons chopped capers

2 tablespoons minced parsley
1 teaspoon lemon juice
⅛ teaspoon Tabasco
1 pound lump crab meat
3 hard-cooked egg yolks
1 pimiento, julienne-cut

Mix the mustard with a little mayonnaise until smooth, then mix with all the mayonnaise, horseradish, the olives, onions, capers, parsley, lemon juice and Tabasco.

Pick over the crab meat, discarding any cartilage. Toss with half the dressing. Heap into 4-6 shells or ramekins and cover with the remaining dressing. Put the egg yolks through a sieve or Mouli grater and sprinkle on top. Garnish with the pimiento strips.

Serves 4–6.

CRAB-MEAT REMICK

1½ pounds crab meat
1 teaspoon dry mustard
½ teaspoon paprika
½ teaspoon celery salt
⅛ teaspoon Tabasco

½ cup chili sauce
1 teaspoon tarragon vinegar
1¾ cups mayonnaise
6 slices crisp bacon

Pick over the crab meat, discarding any cartilage.

Mix together the mustard, paprika, celery salt and Tabasco. Blend in the chili sauce and vinegar, then the mayonnaise.

Heap the crab meat into 6 buttered individual shells or ramekins. Place in a preheated 350° oven for 5 minutes, then top with bacon.

Spread the warmed crab meat with the sauce and place under the broiler until browned. Serves 6.

SCALLOPED OYSTERS AND ARTICHOKES, NEW ORLEANS STYLE

1½ cups cracker crumbs
¾ cup fresh bread crumbs
¾ cup (1½ sticks) butter, melted
¾ teaspoon salt
¼ teaspoon freshly ground black pepper
½ cup chopped chives or green onions

3 tablespoons chopped parsley
1½ pints shucked oysters
½ cup heavy cream
1 package frozen artichoke hearts, cooked and drained

Mix together the cracker crumbs, bread crumbs, butter, salt, pepper, chives and parsley. Drain the oysters, reserving the liquid. Pick over the oysters to remove any shells. Mix oyster liquid and cream. In a 1½-quart buttered baking dish, spread a thin layer of the crumb mixture. Arrange half the oysters over it, then half the artichokes, and sprinkle with half the cream mixture. Cover with half the remaining crumbs, the remaining artichokes, remaining oysters, liquid and remaining crumbs. Bake 25 minutes or until browned and bubbling.

Serves 6–8.

DEVILED CRAB MEAT

2 tablespoons butter
2 tablespoons flour
1 cup light cream
1 pound cooked or canned crab meat, flaked
4 tablespoons chopped onions

4 tablespoons chopped green pepper
1 tablespoon prepared mustard
1 teaspoon Worcestershire sauce
4 drops Tabasco
1¼ teaspoons salt
4 tablespoons bread crumbs

Melt the butter in a saucepan and blend in the flour. When smooth, slowly add the cream, stirring to the boiling point. Cook over low heat 5 minutes.

Mix in the crab meat, onions, green pepper, mustard, Worcestershire and Tabasco sauces, salt and bread crumbs. Taste for seasoning. Spoon the mixture into 6 individual buttered baking dishes, ramekins or shells. Bake in a 400° oven 10 minutes or until delicately browned.

Serves 6.

OMUKO-KAIMORI (Japanese Minced Clams)

3 7½-ounce cans minced clams
Bottled clam juice
1 tablespoon cornstarch
1 tablespoon soy sauce

¼ cup minced green onions
1 cup tiny green peas, cooked or canned
¼ cup chopped water chestnuts

Drain the clams and measure the juice; add enough bottled clam juice to make 1 cup. Mix together the cornstarch, soy sauce, and clam juice. Cook over low heat, stirring constantly, until thickened. Mix in the green onions, peas, water chestnuts, and clams. Divide among 8 shells or ramekins. Bake in a 425° oven 10 minutes.

Serves 8.

BAKED OYSTERS

1 pint shucked oysters
½ cup minced onions
½ cup chopped mushrooms
5 tablespoons butter
2 tablespoons flour
1 cup light cream

2 teaspoons prepared mustard
1 teaspoon Worcestershire sauce
Dash Tabasco
½ teaspoon salt
2 teaspoons minced parsley
¼ cup fine bread crumbs

Pick over the oysters to remove any shells. Sauté the onions and mushrooms in 3 tablespoons of the butter for 3 minutes. Blend in the flour, then add the cream, stirring steadily to the boiling point. Cook over low heat 3 minutes. Blend in the mustard, Worcestershire sauce, Tabasco, salt and parsley, then add the oysters. Cook 1 minute, stirring almost constantly. Taste for seasoning.

Divide mixture among 8 buttered scallop shells or individual baking dishes. Sprinkle with the bread crumbs and dot with the remaining butter. Bake in a preheated 400° oven 15 minutes.

Serves 8.

MOUSSE DE HOMARD (Lobster Mousse, French Style)

1 1½-pound live lobster
2 tablespoons minced onion
2 egg whites

1½ teaspoons salt
⅛ teaspoon Tabasco
2½ cups very cold heavy cream

Remove the meat of the lobster. Blend the lobster meat, onion, egg whites, salt and Tabasco in an electric blender until smooth and fluffy, or chop the lobster to a paste, gradually beating in the onion, egg whites and seasonings. Chill 2 hours, then beat in the cream very well and pour into a 1½-quart buttered mold. Place mold in a pan of hot water, cover the pan and cook over medium heat 40 minutes or until firm. Unmold carefully and serve hot or cold, with crusty bread. Serves 6.

FONDUE (The Swiss National Cheese Dish)

1 clove garlic
1½ cups dry white wine
4 cups (1 pound) grated Gruyère or Swiss cheese (not processed)
2 teaspoons potato flour or cornstarch
3 tablespoons kirsch
¼ teaspoon freshly ground black pepper
French bread

Rub a chafing dish or casserole with the garlic. Pour the wine into it and heat over low heat until bubbles just begin forming around the edges. Mix in the cheese, stirring steadily with a wooden spoon until melted and smooth. Mix the potato flour and kirsch until smooth, then stir into the cheese mixture until bubbly in the center. Stir in the pepper.

To serve, place or keep the dish over an alcohol burner or candle warmer. The fondue should be kept hot, but not bubbling. Cubes of French bread are then dipped with a fork into the fondue by each person. If mixture becomes too thick, blend in a little more wine.
Serves 8–10.

VITELLO TONNATO (Italian Veal in Tuna Fish Sauce)

¼ cup olive oil
4 pounds rolled leg of veal
1 cup sliced onions
1 7¾-ounce can tuna fish, flaked
1 can anchovy fillets, minced
2 cloves garlic
2 bay leaves
½ teaspoon thyme
2 cups dry white wine
1 cup chicken broth
1 orange, in large pieces
½ teaspoon freshly ground black pepper
1½ teaspoons salt
½ cup mayonnaise

Heat the oil in a Dutch oven or heavy saucepan; brown the veal in it. Pour off the fat. Add the onions, undrained flaked tuna fish, anchovies, garlic, bay leaves, thyme, wine, broth, orange, pepper and salt. Cover and cook over low heat 2 hours or until tender. Let cool in the gravy. Remove the veal; discard the bay leaves. Purée the gravy in an electric blender or force through a sieve. Measure 3 cups gravy and gradually mix into the mayonnaise. Slice the veal and pour the gravy over it. Let marinate in the refrigerator at least 4 hours before serving. Garnish with capers.

Serves 10–12.

AVOCADO CUP, CALIFORNIA STYLE

3 avocados
2 tablespoons lime or lemon juices
¼ cup olive or salad oil
2 tablespoons wine vinegar
½ teaspoon salt

⅛ teaspoon Tabasco
1 teaspoon Worcestershire sauce
¼ teaspoon dry mustard
2 tablespoons ketchup

Cut the avocados in half lengthwise and discard the pits. Cut the pulp away from the skin and reserve the shells. Dice the pulp; toss with the lime juice. Beat together the oil, vinegar, salt, Tabasco, Worcestershire sauce, mustard and ketchup. Toss with the avocado. Chill 15 minutes before serving. Heap in the shells.

Serves 6.

PISSALADIÈRE (Onion Pie Provencale)

¼ cup olive oil
4 tablespoons butter
4 cups chopped onions
1 teaspoon salt
½ teaspoon freshly ground black pepper

1 9-inch baked pastry shell
2 cans fillets of anchovies, drained and chopped
1 cup sliced black olives

Heat the oil and butter in a skillet; sauté the onions over very low heat until tender and lightly browned. Season with the salt and pepper. Cool, then spread in the pastry shell.

209

Sprinkle with the anchovies and olives. Bake in a preheated 375° oven 10 minutes. Serve hot.

Serves 6.

BUREK ME PRESH (Leek and Cottage Cheese Pie, Albanian Style)

1¾ cups flour	½ cup milk
1¾ teaspoons salt	1 pound cottage cheese
1 cup water	2 eggs
1½ cups melted butter	⅛ teaspoon freshly ground black
6 leeks or 12 scallions (both white and green part), thinly sliced	pepper

Sift together the flour and 1 teaspoon of the salt. Add the water and mix until a dough is formed. Knead gently. Roll out as thin as possible on a lightly floured surface. Brush the dough with butter and cut into 3-inch squares. There should be about 12. Stack in two piles, 7 in one pile and 5 in the other.

Put 3 tablespoons of the remaining butter in a saucepan and sauté the leeks 5 minutes, stirring frequently. Mix in the milk and cook over medium heat 2 minutes. Beat the cottage cheese, eggs, remaining salt and pepper together and combine with the leek mixture. Mix well.

Roll and stretch the stack of 7 dough squares, still piled on top of each other, until large enough to cover a 9-inch buttered pie plate. Line plate with pastry and fill with cottage cheese-leek mixture. Roll and stretch the stack of 5 squares until it is large enough to cover the top of the pie. Seal edges carefully, pressing with edge of a fork. Brush the top with the remaining butter and bake in a preheated 400° oven 30 minutes. Reduce heat to 325° and bake 15 minutes longer. Cut in wedges, serve hot or cold.

Serves 6–8.

SCANDINAVIAN SMOKED-FISH PANCAKES

Pancakes:

1½ cups sifted flour	1 egg, beaten
½ teaspoon salt	¾ cup water
½ cup milk	3 tablespoons vegetable oil

Sift the flour and salt into a bowl. Beat in the milk until very smooth, then the egg and water. The batter should be thin, so add a little more water if necessary. Let stand 30 minutes.

Heat a 5-inch skillet and brush with oil. Pour in just enough batter to coat the bottom thinly, tilting the pan quickly. Bake until lightly browned on both sides. Stack while preparing the balance of the pancakes and add more oil as needed.

Filling:

¾ pound smoked whitefish, salmon or sturgeon	½ cup chopped onions
	2 hard-cooked eggs, mashed
5 tablespoons butter	1 egg white

Remove any skin or bones of the fish and chop the fish. Melt 2 tablespoons butter in a skillet; sauté the onions 10 minutes. Mix with the fish, hard-cooked eggs and egg white. Taste for seasoning, adding salt and pepper if necessary.

Put some of the mixture on each pancake. Turn opposite sides in and roll up. Melt the remaining butter in a skillet; sauté the rolls in it until browned. Serve hot or cold.

Makes about 16; serves 8.

BOQUITAS DE FRIJOLES (Black Bean Appetizer, Puerto Rican Style)

1 cup dried black beans	3 tablespoons olive oil
2 onions	Vegetable oil for deep frying
3 cloves garlic	6 slices toast, trimmed and quartered
4 cups water	
1 teaspoon salt	¼ cup grated Parmesan cheese

Wash the beans well and soak overnight in water to cover. Drain and wash again. Put in a saucepan with 1 onion, the garlic and water and cook over medium heat 2 hours, or until beans are soft. Purée in an electric blender or rub through a sieve. Mix in the salt.

Chop the remaining onion. Heat the oil in a saucepan and cook the chopped onions, and puréed beans, stirring constantly, until thick, about 5 minutes. Taste for seasoning.

Heat the vegetable oil to 375° and drop in bean mixture by the heaping teaspoon. Fry until they rise to the surface, about 2 or 3 minutes. Drain. Arrange on the toast and sprinkle with the cheese. Serves 6.

PISTO (Mixed Vegetable Appetizer, Italian Style)

1/3 cup olive oil
3 cups chopped onions
2 cloves garlic, minced
2 tablespoons minced parsley
4 red or green peppers, sliced
1 pound tomatoes, peeled
  and chopped

1 pound yellow squash or eggplant,
  peeled and diced
1½ teaspoons salt
¾ teaspoon freshly ground black
  pepper

Heat the oil in a deep skillet; sauté the onions, garlic and parsley in it for 10 minutes. Mix in the peppers; cover and cook over low heat 10 minutes. Add the tomatoes, squash or eggplant, salt and pepper. Cook 30 minutes longer, stirring frequently. Serve cold.

Serves 4–6.

RATATOUILLE PROVENCALE (Vegetable Appetizer, Provence Style)

1 1½-pound eggplant
3 green peppers
2 large onions
1 small zucchini
½ cup olive oil

3 tomatoes, diced
2 teaspoons salt
½ teaspoon freshly ground black
  pepper
2 cloves garlic, minced

Peel the eggplant and cut in small dice. Cut the peppers in strips; slice the onions and zucchini very thin.

Sauté each of the vegetables (but the tomatoes) separately, in 1 tablespoon oil for each, 5 minutes. In a casserole arrange successive layers of the sautéed vegetables and the tomatoes, sprinkling each layer with salt, pepper and garlic. Add the remaining oil. Cover and bake in a 350° oven 1¼ hours. Watch carefully and add a little boiling water if necessary to keep from burning. Serve hot or cold.

Serves 8.

STUFFED PEPPER APPETIZER SALAD

6 green peppers
½ cup olive oil
2 tablespoons wine vinegar
1 teaspoon salt
¼ teaspoon pepper
½ teaspoon dry mustard
¼ pound cheddar cheese, diced
¼ pound Swiss cheese, diced

Cover the green peppers with water. Bring to a boil and cook 5 minutes. Drain, cool, and cut in half, removing the seeds and membranes. Chill.

Beat together the oil, vinegar, salt, pepper and mustard. Add the cheddar and Swiss cheeses. Marinate 30 minutes. Stuff the pepper halves with the cheese mixture. Serve on lettuce leaves.

Serves 12.

OEUFS À LA RUSSE (Eggs, Russian Style)

1 cup mayonnaise
3 tablespoons chili sauce
1 tablespoon chopped green olives
1 tablespoon chopped chives or green onions
1 teaspoon chopped parsley
Dash Tabasco
2 teaspoons lemon juice
6 hard-cooked eggs, halved lengthwise

Mix together all the ingredients but the eggs. Arrange 2 egg halves, cut side down, on each of 6 small plates. Cover with the sauce. Garnish with watercress or shredded lettuce.

Serves 6.

GALANTINE DE DINDE (Turkey Galantine, French Fashion)

12-15 pound turkey
1 pound ground lean veal
1 pound ground lean pork
1 pound salt pork, cubed
1 cup heavy cream
¼ cup cognac
2 teaspoons salt
¾ teaspoon freshly ground black pepper
1 teaspoon nutmeg
½ teaspoon thyme

½ pound unsalted fatback, cut into strips
½ pound cooked tongue, cut into strips
2 truffles, sliced
¾ cup pistachio nuts or sliced almonds
2 carrots
1 stalk celery
1 sprig parsley

Have the turkey boned by the butcher or do it yourself. Using a sharp knife, remove all the meat from the skin, being careful not to pierce the skin. Reserve meat and the skin. Cook the bones in 2 quarts salted water for 2 hours. Strain and reserve the stock.

Cut the breast and drumstick meat into small cubes. Grind together the remaining turkey meat, the veal and lean pork. Combine with the salt pork, cream, cognac, salt, pepper, nutmeg and thyme.

Lay the turkey, skin outside, down on a flat surface and spread with the turkey mixture. Arrange alternate rows of fatback, tongue and truffles. Sprinkle with the nuts. Pull the edges of the skin together to form a sausagelike roll and carefully sew the edges of the skin.

Heavily butter a few layers of cheesecloth and place the galantine on it. Roll it tightly and tie at ends and in the middle, keeping the roll even and smooth. Place the roll in a large saucepan and add the vegetables and enough of the reserved broth to cover. Cover the pan, bring to a boil and cook over low heat 1½ hours. Let the galantine cool in the liquid. Remove it from the broth.

Carefully unroll the galantine and reroll it in a clean cloth. Weight it down with a heavy plate for 3 hours, then remove the cloth. Remove the thread from the skin. The galantine may be decorated with Sauce Chaud Froid or an aspic made from the broth in which the turkey was cooked mixed with gelatin. Chill and cut into thin slices. Serve as a first course with buttered toast.

Serves 12–15.

STUFFED EDAM CHEESE, CURACAO STYLE

1 whole 4-pound Edam cheese	Dash cayenne pepper
2 tablespoons butter	1½ cups peeled chopped tomatoes
1 cup minced onions	½ cup dry bread crumbs
1 pound ground beef	2 eggs, beaten
1 teaspoon salt	½ cup chopped stuffed olives

Leave the wax coating on the cheese. Cut a 1-inch horizontal piece off the top. Scoop out the cheese, leaving a half-inch-thick shell. Cover shell with water and let soak 1 hour. Drain. Grate enough of the scooped-out cheese to measure 2 cups.

Melt the butter in a skillet; sauté the onions 5 minutes. Add the meat; cook over medium heat 5 minutes, stirring frequently. Add the salt, pepper and tomatoes; cook 5 minutes. Remove from heat and mix in the bread crumbs, eggs, olives and grated cheese. Stuff the cheese and replace the top. Wrap tightly in foil or, preferably, cheesecloth. Place in a deep pan, as some of the red wax will melt during baking. Bake in a 375° oven 1 hour. Remove from pan and let stand 5 minutes. Peel off the outer wax skin, cut into wedges, and serve.

Serves 6–8.

Note: Cooked flaked fish or diced cooked chicken may be substituted for the beef.

ROULADE AU PÂTÉ (French Pâté Roll)

4 cups mashed potatoes
4 egg yolks, beaten
4 tablespoons flour
4 egg whites, beaten stiff
5 3¼-ounce cans pâté de foie gras
Pimiento strips

Grease an 11 by 17-inch jelly-roll pan; line it with wax paper and grease again.

Beat together potatoes, egg yolks and flour, taste for seasoning, then fold in the egg whites thoroughly. Spread in the prepared pan. Bake in a preheated 375° oven 20 minutes or until a cake tester comes out clean. Cool, then turn out onto a towel; carefully peel the paper off the bottom. Cut in half lengthwise.

Mix the pâté until smooth, then spread half on each potato cake. Roll up like a jelly roll. (Don't worry if it cracks in rolling.) Heat in the oven or serve cold, decorated with pimiento strips. Cut in half-inch slices.

Serves 8–12.

Variation: Caviar Roulade

Spread rolls with sour cream, red or black caviar, sieved hard-cooked egg yolks and minced onions. Roll up. Serve cold, with additional sour cream.

INDEX

221

225

228

230

234

235

238

MORE PAPERBACK LIBRARY
EASY-TO-COOKBOOKS
By Ted and Jean Kaufman ...

__COOKING FOR TWO (54-671, 75¢)

__LOW-COST GOURMET COOKING (53-571, 60¢)

__GRANDMOTHER'S COUNTRY COOKBOOK
(55-381, 95¢)

__ITALIAN COOKING MADE EASY (54-791, 75¢)

__THE COMPLETE BREAD COOKBOOK
(65-143, 95¢)

You Will Also Enjoy ...

__THE GOURMET HEALTH FOODS COOKBOOK
by Mike and Olga Teichner (64-222, 75¢)

__TASTY COOKING FOR ULCER DIETS
by Orlena Aagaard (65-079, 95¢)

__THE WEEKEND CHEF
by Carol Truax (65-073, 95¢)

__AUTHENTIC SPANISH COOKING
by Maruja Hatheway (64-061, 75¢)

__THE YOGA COOKBOOK
by Edna Thompson (64-012, 75¢)

__BARBECUES
by Mark and Roberta Ames (53-795, 60¢)

__THE BURGER COOKBOOK
by Ruth Ellen Church (53-794, 60¢)

__THE BEGINNERS' COOKBOOK
by Hyman Goldberg (55-739, 95¢)

If you are unable to obtain these books from your local
dealer, they may be ordered directly from the publisher.

PAPERBACK LIBRARY

Department B

315 Park Avenue South

New York, N.Y. 10010

Please send me the books I have checked.

I am enclosing payment plus 10¢ per copy to cover
postage and handling.

Name ....

Address .. ..

City .... State .... Zip Code ....

_____ Please send me your free mail order catalog